FRAN

by Moe Kornbluth

This book is dedicated to Fran Justa.
She was its inspiration and the center of my life.

I must thank
John McCaffrey,
Corrie Dosh,
Frank Haberle,
Liza Bolitzer,
Phil Miller,
Melinda Burke
and Stan Miller
for their supportive encouragement
and constructive advice.

Author's Email: moecsba@earthlink.net

ISBN: 978-0-578-12495-7

FORWARD

To anyone who has seen the Academy Award-winning movie *A'mour*, Morris Kornbluth's Fran is immediately recognizable. It is a love story. Unlike *A'mour*, however, it is not so much the story of a husband struggling with his wife's decline, but the story of the remarkable and heroic woman he married and for whom he is now the principal caregiver.

I first met Fran Justa 25 years ago, in 1988, when I joined The Dime Savings Bank of New York as its President. At the time, Fran was President of Neighborhood Housing Services of New York and we, The Dime, were one of her supporting banks. NHS, as it was called, was one of those New York City-based non-profits formed during the 1960's designed to pick up where government left off. In NHS's case, the mission was to help assure adequate housing opportunities for low and moderate-income families in the New York metropolitan area.

While NHS may have been but one of a number of housing-oriented agencies operating in New York, Fran was anything but the typical agency leader. When it came to representing the interests of poor and vulnerable people—and seeing to it that they had adequate and equitable access to decent and affordable housing—Fran was a demon! There was no obstacle too large, no opponent too formidable, no task too great for Fran to tackle. Under her leadership, NHS became not just a force, but the force, in the affordable housing movement of the day.

But, of course, Fran was more than just a visionary leader. She was a wife and mother, a friend to countless numbers, and an engaged and committed member of the wider community. To know her and be invited into her world, was to be swept up in her passion for and commitment to social justice.

Fran Justa is a true hero; to me and to many others who knew her, worked with her and supported her efforts. Principal among those is her husband, Moe, whose reflections on this remarkable woman, and on their life together, you are about to read.

Dick Parsons

INTRODUCTION

There are remarkable people who can literally change the world and the lives of those they interact with. They are altruistic, have unbounded energy, great enthusiasm, optimistic vision, tremendous work ethic, and a belief in justice and fairness. They can instill hope, provide support, enable happiness and satisfaction in others. Fran Justa is one of these people.

I'm telling this story for several reasons. First, to reacquaint myself with my past, to try to understand what's happened to me over the years, and to learn some truths about who I am. I also want to share my experiences so that others may be better prepared for difficult times, when life "blindsides" you, as it has a way of doing, making you change long-held plans, when the expected becomes the unexpected.

The usual idea is to start a story from the beginning and follow a straight narrative line to the finish. But I want to do this differently, taking you on a road with many turns, detours, dead ends, cul-de-sacs and rotaries. (Don't you love the traffic analogy?) Life is much the same. There are times of growth and other times retractions. We are organic creatures. We have an impact on the people around us, on our surroundings, and they on us. It is up to us to decide what to do on this journey called life—what we want to achieve, experience, or leave behind.

In 1998 Fran, at the age of 56, was diagnosed with Parkinson's Disease. Her illness had a major impact on our journey as a couple, and on myself, but it took me 10 years to fully understand just how much. In many ways, Parkinson's became our relationship, that terrible decade when I struggled to deal with Fran's illness, as it threatened to wipe out the wonderful 30 years we had before. I was beginning to forget what we had been like when Fran was healthy, all we had been through together, all the laughter, the special moments, the good times. This, then, is the true reason I am writing this book…to remember.

Fran (Francine) Justa, Bat Mitzvah, 1954

Moe (Morris) Kornbluth, Bar Mitzvah, 1952

CHAPTER 1

My name is Moe and my wife's name is Fran. On June 24th, of 2011 we celebrated our 40th wedding anniversary. We met when she was 28 and I was 31. We fell in love (whatever that is) or heat (I know what that is). It was a whirlwind romance and we were married eight months after we met. It's all about the chemistry or the poetry.

Back in 1970 Fran was dating Joe Simons, my oldest and closest friend, and they were breaking up. I had met her twice, at social gatherings of friends. Shortly after the breakup she contacted a mutual friend of ours and asked him to find out if I would go out with her. I was surprised and called Joe to find out what was going on in their relationship. He told me they were no longer dating and that I should go out with her. He praised her without reservation. He said, "She is a wonderful person. Enjoy her."

Fran and Joe (my best friend), Fire Island, 1970

We set up our first date on Halloween of 1970. Six of us went to Chinatown. We went in my friend Manny Weiss's car, the only one of us who had an automobile. Fran and I hit it off immediately. In the ride to the restaurant we sat jammed against each other and we were attracted like magnets. We kept touching each other throughout the night, playfully and sensually. Manny drove us back to her apartment and I saw her to her door, as any gentleman would. She invited me in (supposedly) to see her apartment. I didn't realize she wasn't going to let me out of there. After awhile Manny rang the bell and Fran answered the intercom and told him, "He's not coming down."

It must have been clear right away that Fran and I were enthralled with each other…and greatly amorous. After that first night together we went the next morning to a neighborhood diner. We had the standard Sunday morning breakfast and when we had finished eating the waitress approached our booth and stood before us looking very serious. She said, "This meal is going to be very expensive!" "Why is that?" I asked. She said, "There is a love tax!" And that is how it began. (I learned later that Fran told her friend Leah after our first night that I was the one for her and that she was going to marry me. A gut reaction that paid off!)

I moved in with Fran not long after our first date and seven months later we were married. I didn't feel the need to get married. I was committed to Fran but she wanted to do it and when a guy is in love he does anything for his gal. So we got married.

Let me tell you the details because that sets the tone of our life. We talked things out and made decisions together. We could always talk things out and if we didn't agree we could still support the outcome when we realized the importance of an issue to either of us. Our trusting each other was the major strength in our relationship. We trusted each other without reservation. We also never had a problem with sharing. We shared everything from pasta dishes to bank accounts to germs. Our wedding was fun and intimate. My friend Joe took the photo that I developed and printed for our announcement. Only the most important people in our lives were invited. That came to about 19 people. Some of my friends and some of Fran's and some that we had mutually. We also invited our shrink but that's another story. Fran's parents, her Uncle Howard and Aunt Lee, were also there. My brother Phil came, but that's it from my family, as they did not approve our decision to be married by a minister from the Ethical Culture Society. Fran's friend Sonny supplied the food, one of our friends wrote a song for us, and we wrote the vows, spending several days trying to come up with the most perfect words to express our love for each other and our hopes for the future.

The reception was also a cool event. We rented a bus and invited about 60 people to spend the day at a summerhouse we shared with four other couples on Fire Island. Uncle Howard provided all the food as a wedding present and the gods provided a beautiful sunny day. Things started out really well—no friction. That was how we managed much of our life together. We did things together. We wanted to be together. Our bond was a very visceral and physical attraction at the start, and then it lasted.

CHAPTER 2

My maternal grandfather came to this country from Poland after World War I. His name was Baruch. He came from a backwater community in middle Europe with peasant roots and was not an educated man. But he was fiercely religious and I believe this is the basis for his humanity, civility, morality and ethics. When he reached these "golden shores" he did not have an occupation. He settled in the lower east side of Manhattan where many of his countrymen landed before him and where there were some support services. As I learned about the story, one day while walking through his neighborhood, Baruch saw a sign noting a business for sale. It was a bakery. He entered the store and met with the owner. He asked the owner if the business was a good business.

"Does it make a profit?"

"Yes," the owner said. "It's a very good business and a good living."

Baruch then asked if the business could support a family, as he had two sons he planned to bring over from Poland along with his wife and daughter.

"It certainly can support them all as it has done for me," the owner replied.

It sounded good to Baruch, except one problem: he wasn't a baker.

"Can you teach me the business? Do you think I can learn it?"

The owner told him that he could help him and that he had workers who would stay and work for him and teach him all he had to know.

"If all that is true," said Baruch. "If you will teach me the business and it can support my family and it is doing well I would like to buy it from you. But right now I don't have the money to pay you. But since the business will do well and is profitable, if you agree, I will pay you from those profits."

The owner agreed. They shook hands to finalize the deal. And that is how my family became the owners of a bakery on the lower east side of Manhattan where my parents and uncles lived and worked.

My grandfather Baruch saved his money and after several years was able to bring all the members of his immediate family to the States. This is where my parents met. My father had very little schooling but he was versed in Hebrew and Yiddish. My mother went to public school and always enjoyed the activity of learning. When I was ready to enter school we moved to Williamsburg, Brooklyn. That was where a Yeshiva of high quality was located. With that move my parents stopped working for my grandfather. My mother got a job in a different bakery in the neighborhood, while my father became a painter of house interiors.

A proper education for their children was of major importance to my parents. I was in school all day. Religious studies were in the morning and secular classes were held in the afternoon and lasted till 6 P.M. The most important thing in my parent's lives was their religion. It encompassed and controlled all aspects of their being, from waking to going to sleep, every day, in all activities. This heritage was what they wanted to pass along to their offspring. I had a sister, Toby, who was three years older than I, and a brother, Philip, who was seven years younger. Our household was warm and supportive. My parents weren't consumers. They were careful how they spent their earnings, similar to many who grew up during the Great Depression of the 1930's. But we never went hungry and never felt we did without.

I don't know what determines and controls the turns and twists that make up our lives. What impacts and molds ones character and personality. Consider that my brother and sister and I grew up in the same household under the same religious structures. My family was strictly kosher and Sabbath observers. We also observed all Jewish holidays, while secular holidays had no meaning or significance in our lives. Yet by the time I was 20 the religion no longer seemed meaningful and it couldn't hold me. Basically, it didn't seem to make sense to me or was reasonable that there were so many different gods who played favoritism with so many different groups of people. So I dropped it. But every once in a while my background jumps up and surprises me. The rigidity of the religion that was in my bones still lingers but I do not let it overcome me.

I wasn't aware how much I had hurt my parents by not staying religious. I tried to explain to my mother my reasons for not being observant, but she really couldn't accept them. I could not talk to my father about this issue at all. He would just walk away from me. I didn't understand until much later that their pain was in that they had worked so hard trying to make me into the best person they could, which meant an observant Jew, and I had rejected their efforts. At least I think that's what caused the pain. But even with that I would not change my parents for anything. They were kind, generous, warm people. Our house was always open to people in need. They had good values. They were ethical and moral people and I believe that I retained these qualities. Still, I believe that religious indoctrination can make someone irrationally stubborn and emotionally rigid. My background sometimes catches me unawares and can color my responses and actions. Happily, I can sometimes see the error of my ways. It just takes too long to change.

CHAPTER 3

Fran's upbringing was different from mine. She was born in Richmond, Virginia. When she was a very young girl her father left the family. Fran, I think, blamed herself for his disappearance. Her mother never explained what had happened or gave Fran letters from her father that he sent and addressed to her after he left. It haunted her childhood. Fran told me that when playing in her backyard she would sometimes see planes passing overhead and think, "That is my father coming back home." In reality, Fran didn't see him again until she was about 20. Her aunt Dora told her he was dying of emphysema in a Las Vegas hospital and that he would like to see her before he passed.

I can understand how traumatic it must have been for Fran, as a young child, to have her father leave, and then, when finally having the chance to reconnect, learning that he was dying. It must have made her feel terribly sad and insecure. Perhaps, this set her on a path of wanting and working to be accepted by the people she encountered, especially authority figures. It also presented her with an inner conflict because she wanted to be seen as their equal. This impacted many of her relationships with employers and employees, and maybe even friends and acquaintances.

Anyway, after her father left, Fran's mother struggled both economically and socially. It was difficult for a single mother in the South in the 1940's. Being Jewish in that community also didn't endear you to your classmates or neighbors. Jews were considered somewhat better than Negroes, but not by much. Fran told me of the problems and experiences she faced as a Jewish kid without a father growing up in Richmond. She said it was difficult, almost torturous, being excluded from many social activities. She did say that her Hebrew School experiences were joyous. She remembers the names of her Rabbi and Cantor and loved the care and accolades they showered on her whenever she did well. And she tried to do well for them. She always documented her "achievements" or retained evidence of them. What I mean to say is she saved everything besides the standard fare of birth certificate and social security card. She saved her report cards from public school and high school.

Throughout all the years that we have been together, whenever she received a greeting card or letter she would save it and the envelope. When she was 14 years old she weighed 104 pounds and was 61 inches tall. Her general health was good and her vision was 20/20. How do I know all this? Because she saved a copy of the physician's certificate of physical fitness, given to her when she was still a minor and applying for a job in Richmond. She also saved a newspaper job classified ad from The New York Times, yellow with age and taped to an index card, along with the letter she sent to a PO Box applying for her first job when she came to New York City. She has a folder where she saved the cards she received in 1984 from family, friends, and neighbors congratulating her on her graduation for her PhD. Now that's obsessive!

While Fran was still attending high school the firm where her mother was employed relocated to Miami Beach. And so that's where they moved. Being uprooted from familiar surroundings was difficult for Fran, but the change was good as her experiences in Miami were very different from those in Richmond. To start, there was a large Jewish population in Miami and she was readily welcomed by her classmates, many of whom were also Jewish. Entering the high school as a junior must not have been easy with friendships and groups already coalesced, but Fran was a "joiner" and she worked hard at being accepted. The only record I have of her attending Miami Beach High is her graduating class yearbook from 1960. It was called "Typhoon" and had 254 pages. There were about 510 graduating students that year. Fran's interests were listed as "Jr. Red Cross, Dean's Asst., Cheerleader, and French Club." Ever thoughtful and considerate, she lists as her favorite quote: "Don't flatter yourself that friendship authorizes you to say unkind things to your neighbor."

Most of Fran's friend's inscriptions in her yearbook reflect a genuinely positive feeling toward her. You know how difficult and obnoxious teenagers can be to one another, but her classmates spoke highly of Fran, describing how helpful she was and noting her positive attitude, grace, and thoughtfulness. There were no snide remarks or underhanded compliments. They were straight-up laudatory about her. Here's a few to show you what I mean:

Toya—'You can brighten up any room with your refreshing personality.'

Jackie—'Your friendship was a blessing.'

Linda—'Friendly, funny, sweet, and adorable.'

Della—'You are a wonderful girl and one of the sweetest I've ever known.'

Judy—'Usually it takes time to adjust when one transfers, but not you. Without completing one year you made the cheerleading squad and became one of the most loved personalities to grace the halls of Beach.'

After graduating, Fran enrolled at the University of Florida at Gainsville. Before she could settle in to this new and anticipated part of her life her mother became ill and was diagnosed as having a nervous breakdown. This would have a profound impact on Fran, as once again she was uprooted from the familiar and her life disarranged with a dreaded future before her.

CHAPTER 4

After her mother's breakdown, Fran packed up the family car and drove her north to New York, to Brooklyn, where her mother's only living relative, her brother Howard, lived. According to Fran, it was a difficult and harrowing drive as her mother kept trying to get out of the moving car. She tells of having to tie the doors of the car shut so her mother couldn't get out. When they finally arrived in Brooklyn, her mother was institutionalized at Kings County Psychiatric Hospital and Fran moved in with her Uncle Howard.

Needing to work, Fran found a job not long after at May's Department Store in downtown Brooklyn as a sales trainee. That is where she met the man who would become her first husband. I imagine she thought marrying would enable her to start her own life and give her autonomy. Their wedding was on September 19, 1962. She was 20 years old.

The marriage lasted three and a half years. It was a difficult time for Fran, as her first husband was violent, controlling, and physically abusive. She was frightened and threatened by his outbursts. He was very demanding. "Nothing I did would ever satisfy him," she said about the relationship. He broke her nose on one occasion and toward the end of their marriage she was constantly covering up bruises and black and blue marks with makeup and clothing to avoid embarrassment. Finally, she decided to leave him. She went to Mexico to finalize the divorce. It was granted by the "Judicial Power of The State of Chihuahua" on February 2, 1966. Fran kept copies of the divorce papers, in Spanish and in English, along with a notarized letter from the American consulate in Ciudad Juarez as witness to the legality of the proceedings. The notary fee was listed as $2.50. (I told you she saves everything, although often filed in no particular order.)

Fran, you should know, does everything by the book. On April 3, 1966 she went to a rabbi to be released from the marriage in the traditional Jewish way by having the marriage annulled by a practice known as "get." And so a terrible marriage and difficult time in her life was brought to a conclusion in a way that completely satisfied her. All the "I's" were dotted and the "T's crossed, as they say. My feeling is that Fran does things so carefully because she is afraid that she may be caught in a lie, something that has always terrified her. But perhaps this fear is what has made her so honest and trustworthy in all her relationships. Also, wanting to be known as "lily white" might have been a throw back to her southern upbringing. But certainly being "pure" in her relationships was very important to her. Anyway, the divorce left her on firmer ground financially and stronger emotionally, a foundation that would propel her to become the independent, strong-willed women that achieved much success on many levels in her life. But I am getting ahead of myself.

Growing up in Richmond, Fran was surrounded by her maternal grandparents and her father's brother and three sisters. His siblings all adored her father, Louis. I'm not certain about his 20 years separation from Fran other than he was a career enlisted military man. His sister Dora was the one who corresponded with him and kept him informed about family matters. As I mentioned, early on after he left he had written letters (and sent presents) to Fran but she never received any of them, her mother intercepting them and keeping them from her. But her Aunt Dora was instrumental in their reuniting. She was always aware of anniversary dates and birthdays, never missing the opportunity to send a greeting card. She was the family historian and knew that Louis had settled in Las Vegas with his third wife. Fran was at a difficult crossroad in her life at this time. Just divorced and looking for a new job she must have been vulnerable to the suggestions from Aunt Dora to reconnect with her father. And so she did.

They exchanged letters, Fran and her father. In a first letter from her father dated January 20, 1966, he states that they "were very close at just one short period, 1947 to 1951." He acknowledges that he doesn't know Fran at all, but that when she was born it was the most "wonderful thing in the world." He also states that he never stood a chance to keep in contact with her, writing that "you belonged to your mother's side of the family." He also relates Fran's divorce to his own problems with her mother. "You were smart to cut it off rather than endure the agony of repeated arguments," he writes. "A man or woman never changes. The simple problems your mother and I had our first year of marriage stayed with, and multiplied until the divorce. From that I learned not to suffer. So for my second divorce from my Italian wife, when I found it didn't work I didn't wait. Divorce in California was the answer." He then goes on to discuss his latest marriage, his wife Katsuko, his three-week old baby girl, Ida, and how happy he is. He talks about the business his wife and he are starting, "designing, making and selling uniforms to the hotel and casino trade." Overall, the letter seems more about him and his new business, wife and child than any real attempt to connect with Fran. He even signed it: "My Best, Louis." I imagine Fran was upset after reading it. She was still not accepted in the way she needed and perhaps the pain of rejection was felt anew.

On March 18, 1966, Louis sent Fran pictures of his new child, Ida, "The love of my life in her traditional Japanese kimono." He apologizes for the earlier letter saying, "Sorry to be so point blank in my last letter. But I was really taken by surprise for I don't know you...but starting all over again, I will remember I have two daughters." This time he signs, "With affection, Your father & Ida's Papa." He gives and takes away in the same breath.

In a three-page letter dated July 2, 1966, Louis devotes two-thirds of the page describing his business and the equipment and materials he uses. He states that the fabrics he is using for the costumes he makes is not durable enough and asks Fran if she could suggest a fabric or "house" that could furnish him with quality long lasting fabrics. He then reminisces about their past and mentions joys that they shared when she was very young, such as going fishing together and a mutual love of dogs. "Things," he writes, "that your mother couldn't stand." He ends the letter once again expressing the richness in life with a young child. "I can't remember you as a baby as I now see Ida. What a wonderful time in a father's life. To love an infant and have it returned to watch the infant grow into a child and exchange love and affection. To learn to anticipate and recognize her every desire and requirement. To learn to read her face. To see trust or fright, happiness, pleasure, hunger, and determination. Oh yes there is plenty of determination in her face. Just as there was in yours when last I saw you, as you cried in school and you asked me if I had married again. Let me hear from you. Love, Your Father."

The last letter from Louis I found in Fran's files is dated August 9, 1966. In it he once again extols the joys of fatherhood, writing: "If I should die today I feel that I have lived a full life topped off with Ida. I enjoy each day as if it were the last." He encloses some "recent photos of Ida" and again mentions his need for a fabric that is "functional plus beauty and durable. Just what kind of a store is the place you work? Love, Papa."

Just over a year later, on December 5, 1967, Louis died from complications of smoking. I imagine Fran was deeply saddened by his passing, but the feeling must have been complicated given their long estrangement and sporadic reconnection. Perhaps this writing of Fran's, which I found in her files, and is dated December 31, 1993, helps to shed more insight into her complex feelings about her father and family.

Last night in the middle of the night I had a thought that seemed very clear at the time and that now seems muddied but worthy of review. When I was around 6 or 7, my father, who came home every Friday evening from Langley Field Air Force Base and returned every Sunday night, left to go back to the base. It was like every Sunday night, perhaps a bit more exciting because he bought us one of the first TVs in town and it was fun to watch, even if the only thing playing on Channel 6 was Santa Claus reading letters from children.

I didn't know it at the time but that Sunday was to be very different from the rest. He was not coming back. Had I known then I might not have sat in front of the TV but I didn't. On Friday nights when it was warm enough, and Richmond was usually warm enough, I sat out on the front porch and waited for my dad who came in his uniform and rubbed me on the head as he came up the front steps to the house after parking in the driveway behind my Mom's car. I loved the feeling of jumping up and turning into his back as I followed him into the house. Even after that Sunday night when he left for the last time, I waited for him on Friday nights. No one ever told me he wasn't coming back. Sometimes my Mom would say "I don't think your father's coming this week," and I would always answer, "Oh, he'll be here." It always seemed to me that if he weren't going to show, he would have told me. But he didn't tell and he didn't show, and after a few months I just looked out the window, and eventually I stayed in my room on Friday nights. Even today I prefer to stay home or go to Temple on Friday nights. I say to myself it's because it's the end of the week and work has been so stressful and I'm so tired, but I think it has more to do with loss. Better not to anticipate than to lose.

In the middle of last night, it came to me that the way I am, my style, for lack of a clearer thought, is strongly connected to the loss of my father. Oh, I saw him again. Once he visited me in Robert E. Lee Jr. High School for 15 minutes on a Tuesday during the last class before lunch, and then again, one day 13 years later his third wife called me to come down to Las Vegas when he was dying. I went. We talked for two days as best you can when one of the two is dying and talks with no teeth and very little breath, and I thought we had reconciled.

But last night, at 4:15 a.m. I knew I had not yet come to terms with the loss, even if there was a reconciliation. I always thought that most of my reticence to be completely straightforward, or brutally frank as I like to call it, was based on the fears I have resulting from being beaten by my mother, with a shoe; my father, with a belt; and my first husband, with a fist. In fact, after I was hospitalized with a broken nose, broken when my first husband pushed my face into a wall the night John Kennedy was elected President, I thought that my fear of loud voices or of angry men or of sudden movements was all from physical abuse and I talked it out in therapy for 15 years.

This morning though, I realized that most of that abuse came after I was 10 and I remember thinking that nothing anybody could do to me could compare with my father leaving, nothing. In fact, I used to say to my mother when she hit me really hard, "there is nothing you can do to touch me, nothing. You can hit me and bruise my body, but you can't get to me." I was already gotten to.

The revelation made me aware that I too had abandoned my sister, my father's child from a later marriage. My father had three marriages, my mother, a woman in Italy and a Japanese woman. Ida and Debbie were from that marriage and I met Ida at the funeral, Debbie was not yet born, and both of them a few years later. Ida was the oldest child. When she was 12 she got into trouble. She was found in bed with a twenty year old in a model apartment in a building in downtown Las Vegas, where she lived with her mother and her mother's husband.

Her mother, fed up with Ida's behavior sent Ida to live with us and she stayed for 3 weeks. She was beautiful and boys loved her. She went back when she found the rules were too strict in our house.

We lost touch until my Aunt Dora told me that Ida was married. Ida sent me pictures and I called and then a few years later I found out her husband had AIDS. They were poor and lived with his mother in a tiny apartment. His mother was also on disability. We spoke for a few months and lost touch again.

I called a few times but they had moved and there was no forwarding phone number. I called Aunt Dora and got a new number. I called this morning. She's divorced now. It was final last week. She speaks to him sometimes. He's dying. She doesn't have AIDS yet and thinks she won't get it. Even in the year they had sex before she knew he had AIDS, he always pulled out. She didn't use a diaphragm. He didn't use condoms. It's been 4-1/2 years now. She gets tested every six months.

She left waitressing and is working in childcare for $800 a month. She pays $475 rent. She got a GED and a boyfriend who's an assistant manager of a Shoprite. I offered to pay for her courses if she wanted to go back to school at night. She cried. Yesterday was her birthday. She wants to be a teacher. She's 28.

We talked about our father. He died when she was two. She heard only wonderful things about him from her mother. When she was sent to us at 12, she thought I seemed angry with him but she never asked me because she didn't want to deal with it. I told her that he left when I was 6 or 7. I heard only awful things about him from my mother. I told her about the bike he sent to me, silver with brightly colored rubber bands stretched against the spokes. Beautiful but three sizes too small for me. She told me that everyone loved his personality. People laughed when he spoke. I got choked up and my words came out blocked and choppy. She and her mother were going to the cemetery to see him on Sunday. They went every year around the anniversary of his death. She said she loved me. I said I loved her. We stayed on the phone without talking. I had a sudden rush to get off. We hung up. I held the phone in my hand after the click. I think she did too.

I'm skipping around a bit (didn't I warn you), but let me get back to Fran's early life in New York. While she was still with her first husband, she left May's Department Store and got a job as an executive secretary to the president of Holly Stores. There she met Leah Weisburd, someone who was to become her lifelong friend. I always love the story Leah tells about meeting Fran for the first time. Here it is, in Leah's words:

I first saw Fran when I came to work at Holly Stores. The man I was hired to work for had been in an auto accident and would be out for several weeks. They sent me to Fran to help out with the other executive departments. I walked into her office and there was this petite pretty gal with a teased up hair do sitting behind this big desk with tons of papers all over it. She looked up and asked me if I could type and did I know how to deal with numbers and columns. I said yes and then she had the nerve to hand me four documents and say, "I need these back in two hours perfectly done. Can you do that?" The nerve! Here I was trying to help her out and she was snooty to say the least. So I about-faced and returned in one hour with the task complete and perfect. I handed them to her and she looked up at me and said, "I think we will be best friends forever!" And we

Wedding photos

were. We both lived in Brooklyn and we drove into work every day together. Of course I had to call her every morning to wake her up, and she was never ready when I arrived to pick her up. We spent many weekends socializing and she was also responsible for my going into therapy.

Wonderful, right. Clearly, whatever Fran undertook, especially friendships, she did with complete devotion. On the job she worked hard, tried for accuracy, fairness, and thoroughness. She would be loyal to her employer or the organization she was working for and deal honestly and fairly with the employees who reported to her. That was who she was. She also wanted to impress the authority figures in her life with her devotion and reliability.

When I met her she worked as a sales representative for Harvey Probber, an upscale furniture manufacturer. His fame was due to his design of the sectional sofa seating arrangement and furniture that was contemporary and well made. Fran was one of the firm's leading sales people. She sold institutional products mainly to architects and designers.

Honeymoon at Fire Island

CHAPTER 5

When Fran and I met we weren't being very discriminating, or maybe we were subconsciously, about wanting to be together. I thought that any time I could spend with her and didn't was a complete waste. Within a month after meeting I moved in with her. She had a one-bedroom apartment in Manhattan and I had a studio, albeit a large one, in Brooklyn. She didn't want to move to Brooklyn and I saw no problem living in Manhattan. It wasn't too complicated a move. I didn't have much in the way of furniture, so Fran just moved some clothing around and we were comfortable. The furnishings she did have were of good quality and she purchased much of it through the connections she had in her field. She also had two Siamese cats (Sammy and Carlos) she was very fond of. Cats weren't my thing, but what the hell, I thought at the time, you can't have everything, and I might even learn to like them.

Looking back at the past 40 years I don't know the exact right word or words to describe my life with Fran...gamblers might call it "lucky," religious folks "being blessed," and others "good karma." Whatever it is, what we had all these years together is marvelous. Perhaps the best way to describe it is an "addiction." I was addicted to Fran in ways I don't understand. We did have our disagreements and some loud words at times, but it was in the past by the next day and then we wanted to be back together again. That's an addiction and we gratefully had it.

I will offer a thumbnail description of Fran to try and describe what made her so attractive when you would first meet her. Fran was five feet one inch tall and weighed about 120 pounds. She didn't appear threatening. She had a smile that lit up her entire face. Her eyes would glow and sparkle, her face had sincere smile wrinkles and creases, and the temperature in the room would go up by about 10 degrees. Her look was sincere, warm, and inviting. She was physically beautiful, a brunette with a good figure. She also had great rhythm and grace that showed in her walk and when she would dance. She had enough energy for three people. As she grew older and matured, believe me, she became even more attractive as her appearance improved because of her successes and confidence. She was beautiful.

I could speak for both of us but I'll stick to the first person and tell you that when I wake in the morning I am happy she is there and when we sleep at night I love the touch of her skin against mine. We sometimes fall asleep holding hands. She isn't doing well right now, she comes in and out of dementia, but I'll get to that later on. When she is doing well and isn't too much of a difficult person to deal with, I still love being with her. But I am getting ahead of myself.

When we first got together, it wasn't clear to me how many ways Fran and I were different, given that we worked so well together and had this great addiction to each other. We would defer to each other's choice either because we knew of the other's skill or knowledge or just because a strong preference was noted. I'm a sort of laid back guy with a strong backbone and broad shoulders and was able to give in to Fran much of the time without any difficulty. A type "Y" but with a strong will. And Fran, being a type "A" personality, was more demanding and pushy than I was. She was always busy working on something (or many somethings) and would extend herself until she was exhausted and could do no more. She usually had multiple interests going at any one time, while I always try to do one thing at a time or else I become confused.

Anyway, back then I was working a 9 to 5 job and so was Fran. After completing work at Probber, Fran also attended Hunter College. Our apartment was located at the corner of Second Avenue and 38th Street. Fran didn't like to walk home late at night so she would call me after class and I would meet her at the bus stop and we would walk home together. Sometimes we would stay up late working on the school projects or papers she had to complete. I was a better typist than she was at that time and helped her type her papers late into the night. Living in Manhattan had its advantages and drawbacks. It was easy to get to work, but filled with soot and dust. It was an exciting city, something always to do, but also very noisy and chaotic. There were great restaurants, but they were always crowded. You get the drift. However, once Fran and I bonded the things outside of our relationship that had seemed important weren't as attractive. We didn't go to the theatre much, weren't regulars at museums, and didn't bar hop. We did like a good restaurant now and then and would hang out with friends. But Fran's primary interests were work and school, while mine were Fran, work and golf. We were planning for our future and fixing up our little apartment so it was comfortable for two. It was a great time and we had a great time.

CHAPTER 6

In January, 1972 Fran graduated with a BA from Hunter College, summa cum laude. She immediately started on her new educational path that was recommended by one of her customers as a perfect match for her interests. She applied to and was accepted into the Environmental Psychology Program at "The Graduate Center of the City University of NYC", where she, eventually, completed an MA degree at Hunter on September 1976 and continued on for a doctorate at the Graduate Center.

It was about this time that Fran expressed the view, that as a married couple, we should own our own home. This occurred at the same time that I was having a problem with the management agent of our building for illegally charging us a rent that was above market rate. They weren't happy when I presented them with documents showing that the rent we were being charged was illegal and asked for a refund.

We had several good friends and thought it would be great if we could all live in the same vicinity, even in the same building. So we tried to buy a house with several close friends where we could each have our own space and share the expenses. But we could all never agree on a location or type of structure to move into and so that didn't work out. The people in the group therapy sessions we were part of advised us not to move out of Manhattan and not to purchase a multifamily house as we had planned. They expressed that tenants would create problems and headaches one didn't need. We thought that having some rental income would be a good safety net if we were to lose our jobs or wanted to change careers and couldn't work for a while. We also wanted good public transportation, with easy access to our jobs, friends, and nearby shopping. We found all these in Park Slope, Brooklyn. At the time much of the City was being redlined by the banks and property values were down. We were very specific about our needs so we found our house fairly quickly. I think in all we looked at about six houses. The one we decided on was a brick/brownstone type structure that was owner occupied, four-story, three-family, in very good physical condition. The type of building that is standard fare in many urban neighborhoods.

Our next step was to get a mortgage loan. Given that we both had good salaried jobs and good employment records, we figured we were excellent candidates. But once the process started we saw this wasn't the case. We applied for a mortgage at 14 banks and they all turned us down for various reasons, the house was too old, they wouldn't give a mortgage on a three family house, did not like the neighborhood, must be a depositor at the bank for at least six months, too far from a fire house, and on and on and on. The excuses were laughable and should have been criminal because, as we discovered later, when neighborhoods are not invested in they rot and die.

Finally, after receiving a letter of rejection from the Dime Savings Bank Of Brooklyn on Monday, July 20, 1972, I suggested to Fran that, as we had the funds, we buy the building without the bother of getting a mortgage. She was adamant it was not fair, that we should be able to get a mortgage as we never had a credit problem and were not in debt. We had good jobs, were well educated, etc., etc. She did not give up and sought help from the Park Slope Civic Council, an organization whose mission was to improve the neighborhood. The person she spoke to, Everett Ortner, told her to call the Dime Saving Banks. "But they already denied us a mortgage," she said. He told her, "You contacted the wrong person." He gave the name of a different person. So she called the bank again, got the right person, and shortly after we were approved for a mortgage loan in the amount of $26,000 at 7.25 percent interest.

We weren't familiar with the area or community. We were looking at houses and transportation situations that met our immediate needs and not community or social structures. Within walking distance of our home were convenient public transportation, a supermarket, a butcher, a baker, a fruits and vegetables store, a shoe repair, a barber, a tailor, a laundromat, the basics. We didn't notice that on Fifth Avenue between Flatbush Avenue and Union Street, the main shopping thoroughfare, there were many boarded up and abandoned buildings. We were not aware of the crime and drug problems that existed. And the house we purchased was to be delivered vacant. In July of that year we had the house inspected by William J. Klein and the word that resonated throughout his report was "in good condition." We got our mortgage four months later, signed and filed all the required documents, paid the bills and prepared to move in.

There is all this stuff that one has to do before moving physically into a new apartment. Besides packing you have to prepare the new space. Cleaning out all of the old stuff and making it ready for moving in. Luckily, we didn't have very much to do. As I said the house was in very good condition. We took the bottom two floors, a duplex that had a large kitchen and living room on the basement floor and one large study, two small bedrooms and bathroom on the parlor floor. The two rental units were one bedroom floor-throughs. We had all the wood floors sanded and linoleum laid in the kitchen. We put in new kitchens and cabinets and utilities in the tenants' apartments, new carpeting in the hallways, tore down wallpaper and paneling, painted and made other essential improvements. Our duplex required virtually no major changes or work. We sanded floors, removed wallpaper, painted, put up some new light fixtures. Really, not much had to be done. We had ideas about how we wanted the apartments to look and completed the work very quickly. I had boundless energy back then and worked on weekends and evenings for long hours so we could move in and rent the apartments as quickly as possible. At this time Fran was attending graduate school so her schedule was somewhat flexible. We were young and energetic and were certain about our decisions. Some of our new neighbors, we found out later on, watched what we were doing and reported back to the prior owner. I never understood why they did this.

Things worked out rather well. We were able to furnish our two floors with the furniture from our Manhattan apartment. Amazing how much stuff people have. The apartments rented very quickly. Just a note in passing. The top floor was rented to a single man who lived there from 1973 till December 1998. The second floor apartment had one tenant for one year and the second tenant is still living there. Good tenants, good landlord, good karma. No problems.

We learned about the block after we had been living there for a while. It was a quiet block, primarily four-story houses that were inhabited by family units and extended families. There were also five four-story buildings having eight railroad apartments each, three of which were occupied by a mix of low income and welfare tenants.

There were distinct divisions on the block. There were southern Italians, northern Italians, Blacks, Hispanic, some Irish, and the new "hippies," three new families who were considered "pioneers." The people on the block who took an interest in newcomers thought we were crazy to pay $40,000 for a house in this neighborhood. Fran and I were both busy with work and bringing our living situation to a comfortable level. Being friendly we would engage our neighbors in small talk and the few we had contact with were interested in why we purchased our house and what our plans were. We explained that we thought this was a great place to live as it had all the necessary amenities for the comfortable life we were looking for. By the time spring and summer arrived, and people began to hang out on the street, we began to have a different view of our block.

Early photos, 1974–1979

CHAPTER 7

It is quite daunting to consider writing a book covering a period of 40 years without having many written references to rekindle memories to the past. I feel that I am like a camera that is always there taking pictures of a scene but is never in the picture. I never thought I would write this story, and so never gathered and saved the bits and pieces needed to compose it thoroughly. But I believe it is a story worth telling and will do my best to tell it well.

As I said before, in many ways Fran and I are very lucky people. We got along very well, with few major arguments or disagreements. We share similar values, trusted each other, and even though she was independent and successful I was protective of her, both physically and emotionally. I think we had a wonderful marriage. Well a good one anyway. And if you were to ask how I knew that, I would tell of an incident that happened in the locker room at the gym, about two years ago. There were six of us getting dressed after our workouts. One guy complained about his marriage. He said that if he had known what he was getting into he never would have married his wife. He then turned to the rest of us and asked, "If you were to marry again would you marry the same women?" The other four men expressed dissatisfaction with the women they had married. They said they would never have anything to do with them. They seemed bitter and then they turned to me and asked me, "What about you? Would you marry your wife again?" It took me a moment to reply. I thought about it carefully and told them, "I don't know if I would marry her but I certainly would date her."

You see, for the 40 years that I have known Fran, she has been a wonderful person. She was full of energy and alive, she is pretty. She was dynamic, thoughtful, fun to be with, had a sense of humor and a great laugh, she was charming. Even though she was diminutive in height and size she exuded a large energy and confidence and when she entered a room she caused a stir. When she smiled her entire face got into the act. Her eyes would flash and her teeth would sparkle and she was gorgeous. You just knew you could trust her and tell her anything. She could read people and respond to them. Much of the time she preferred to listen to other people rather than talk about herself. And when you spoke to her, you knew you had her attention. Did I tell you she was "very attractive." Men seemed to gravitate to her and she managed them with ease.

Things just aren't the same today as when we started out. But I'll get to that later. Then we were living in Park Slope and Fran's interests and life began to change direction. The problems getting our mortgage had an impact on Fran. I don't know how to tie everything together as so many things happened on this journey. Things may seem out of chronological order and you may have to work a bit to pull it all together but I think it will be worth the effort. I'll try and give you all the pertinent data to make the story understandable.

There we are in early 1973, Park Slope, adding a new branch to the story of our lives. By the time the summer arrived we had settled into our new home, rented the two apartments, and were ready to face whatever came our way. In the summer time is when people came out and congregated on the street. At first Fran was shocked by the number of children and juveniles on the block. They were mostly Black and Hispanic children and they ran wild without supervision, just making a racket and seemed hell bent to cause trouble. The white middle-aged Italian families did not have anything to do with them except to glare and complain. Two different cultures at odds with each other. Initially, Fran was very upset, thinking we had moved into a "slum" and was worried about our safety and the money we had invested. I told her not to be too concerned for if things did not work out we could sell the property or just rent all the apartments and move somewhere else. This, however, turned out to be a divine moment for Fran. It was one of the major turning points in her life. While I was doing the 9 to 5 Fran was working on her studies, which were very time consuming, and she decided to organize the block and make it a better place to be. At this time Fran was no longer at Probber. She had started on her PhD at the CUNY Graduate Center and as the spring of '73 approached, and Carroll Street come alive with people taking advantage of warmer weather, Fran took to the street. She would never hesitate in talking to people. Her sales experience taught and strengthened her so she did not take rejection personally, and she knew how to listen sincerely when other people talked about issues important to them. Being a "people person" she would easily talk to anyone and they to her. She befriended several people who had lived on the block since childhood as well as several new homeowners, "yuppies," as they were called. She quickly found what the dynamic on the block was all about. There were many tenants and homeowners who had lived on the block a long time and their connections were based on ethnic, religious, social, economic, and related sources. Then there were the outsiders. Poorer, maybe welfare, single mothers, wrong ethnic, religious, social and/or economic class or status and they didn't control their children. Fran found out very quickly that the parent or parents of these difficult children lived under difficult circumstances. Some of the families had six or seven children. Some of the single mothers had boyfriends over and to maintain privacy would lock the doors to their children. Fran, deciding she wanted to live on this block, was determined to make it better for all the residents and the way to do this was to start a block association.

Fran is an organizer. Compulsive and detail oriented she managed to organize the first block meeting on February 18, 1973. The meeting was held in Saint Francis Xavier's auditorium and some 60 residents attended to "discuss, among other topics, neighborhood problems and determine how a block association can combat crime." Dues were set at $5 per family to support block activities and pay bills. Committees were set up for senior citizens, young people, security, sanitation, beautification and health care. Everyone at that first meeting signed on to a committee.

The next meeting was scheduled for March 18th and was attended by over 80 people. The guest speaker was Sgt. Tartaglia, Community Affairs Officer for the New York City Police Department. Before giving his speech on what steps to take to ensure safety, reduce crime, and recover stolen property he noted: "I have never seen such a large group of people for any block association meeting I have ever attended." That's Fran. She was so successful because she rang every doorbell on the block, talking to residents, selling them on the block association. Not many people could reject her when she requested that they attend the meetings. She organized the first block party for July 28, 1973 into a success with raffles, a band, pot luck dinner, children rides, plant sale, food and beverages for sale. This was the first party on the block since the one held celebrating the end of World War II. The certificate of incorporation was filed on April 2, 1974 for the Carroll Street Block Association. She was now taking classes towards her PhD and as President of the Carroll Street Block Association, making connections with other civic, social, religious, and community groups to make her block association credible.

I have been trying to understand how Fran was transformed into the person she became or what caused the release of this potential. There was of course a belief in her own abilities that was supported by all she had accomplished in the work place. Being accepted into a graduate program at a recognized quality institution. The purchase of a home that created a sense of stability in her life and grounded her to a community. And with some humility, but perhaps the most important, the strength of our marriage and being with a man she could rely on for unquestioned trust, support, and loyalty. These may have given her the strength to tackle some of the problems she would encounter and those she would recognize that needed her attention.

Carroll Street had problems, but so did Park Slope (or South Brooklyn as some of the old timers called the neighborhood) and the only way to resolve it was through organizing. Throughout her life Fran had learned that you fix things by recognizing that a problem exists, defining it, addressing it with input from many different sources, determining solutions and bringing the resources to bear on the problem. So she talked to the people on the block. Exuding her customary exuberance and energy, she attracted many people with and to her ideas. By the end of the summer there was no person on the block who didn't know Fran and how active and involved a person she was. Our home became a meeting place for adults to discuss problems and for children to relax from the problems that they faced in their homes…even if they just needed the bathroom.

I remember one time, shortly after Fran began getting involved in the problems of the block, coming home and seeing four children, ages six to 12 or so, sitting in the dark on the couches in our living room. I asked Fran, "What's going on?"

"With what?" she replied.

"There are kids sitting in our living room!"

"Oh," she said. "They needed some quiet time. With so many other siblings it is never quiet in their homes. And sometimes their mother locks them out of the house so they can have some privacy. So I let them come here whenever they need to."

Showing my bias I said, "Fran, I don't know if these kids can be trusted. They could steal something, you know."

"No they won't." she said confidently.

And they never did.

Fran was always willing to help someone in trouble without expecting any return on her actions. Jill Friedman, a friend, remembers an incident when her baby daughter got injured and she needed help:

It was one of "those evenings." Ralph was working, Tova was an infant or so, Sarah was anxiously awaiting some festivity at Union Temple. Zoe had banged her head on the tub while taking a bath with me and I was concerned. I could not take Sarah to the Temple so I called Fran. I may have sounded hysterical but Fran's response was anything but.The sound of her cool, calm voice put everything in perspective. "What do you need me to do for you?" And I said without even thinking. "Could you pick up Sarah and take her to Temple?" Fran's calmness reminded me of what really mattered at that moment. "We will be there in 10 minutes." Fran and Moe saved my day.

Fran, now in her first year in a graduate school program, began to figure out how to bring help to Carroll Street and make it a better place to live. Her involvement in grad school provided her with a broader life out-look as she was involved with many course readings that broadened her understanding of how to analyze a problem, figure out what made things work the way they do, and how to address the issue to accomplish the changes needed for the results you want.

CHAPTER 8

Those early years, Fran felt that she was working to make Carroll Street the best possible place to live for all of its residents, be they owners or renters. She was not interested in having people own property on the block who were absentee landlords as they would not have the neighborhood's interest as a major priority. She was president of the block association for three years and then relinquished it to Ann Garzillo, a long time resident. Fran continued to work in the background and was still accepted as the decision maker and leader of the group. Now her interests were directed towards her education and eventual graduate degree. But she could not imagine what events would transpire that grew out of the work to get her degree that would involve her in so many other activities.

At the time I did not realize how her studies transformed her from a savvy young women into an intellectual. Her course work forced her to start thinking logically and to support her results with reasonable, rational arguments and statistical measurements. In some ways she was able to incorporate skills she had learned in the business world and sharpened them for the academic milieu. She was never skilled at math, usually would count to ten on her fingers, and had to take classes in statistics, which she found very difficult to understand, but with the help of other students was able to pass the course.

Of course, Fran took copious notes and maintained files of all the material she had to read or review. I was unaware of the broad scope of knowledge that her education provided. I only recently found this out by going through her papers and was impressed by the diversity of subject matter. From 1972 through 1976 she studied topics such as people's relationship and interaction with their geography, city design and planning, land use studies and urban renewal, sociology, historical and philosophic comparison of nature and human environments, the role of religion in man's decisions, eastern and western societies different concepts of the world, climate influences on issues and decisions, the slum environment, children's environments from playground to classroom, "sex and race norms on personal space," congestion in subway stations, and more. These studies taught her how to think and present her ideas convincingly in an organized and detailed method that lent credibility to her projects and plans.

In 1975 Fran started a major study on a group called "Little Italy Restoration Association." Here she recorded the attempts to set up an organization that needed neighborhood support from many different groups; religious, mercantile, social, and political to be successful. This group faced many difficult organizational problems due to the wants of the different interest groups involved, being unable to get groups to come together for a common cause, and lacking in street recognition. Fran, however, was surprised to see how successful they were in raising funds for projects and staff. She began to recognize and understand the connection between not for profit groups and funding from city, state, federal and private sources. This was a valuable lesson that helped her in every future endeavor. She also began to write in a very erudite, clear and careful manner. Her thoughts were presented in an orderly fashion, with clarity and focus. This she acquired from her studies and it made her better and more capable at whatever she went after.

Her involvement in the community led her out of the structured comfort zone of the Graduate Centers Environmental Psychology Department. She and Tim O'Hanlon, a fellow student, became interested in the impact of change on neighborhoods both physically and financially what caused the stresses to a community and how they might rally. They worked jointly on collecting data and researching and discussing the information they were finding into the early 1980's. This led to a different angle on the environment than was expected from dissertation students in their program and they had to convince their dissertation advisors to accept the concept that political decisions had an effect on urban environments.

Tim's dissertation, completed in 1982, was titled "Neighborhood Change in New York City: A Case Study of Park Slope 1850-1980." Never one to mince words, Fran's dissertation, completed in 1984, was titled: "Effects of Housing Abandonment, Resettlement Processes, And Displacement On The Evolution Of Voluntary Community Organizations In Park Slope, Brooklyn, New York." Her interest in this topic took her to neighborhood and community meetings where she met many residents, merchants and professionals. It was in this role that she was able to get a complete picture of the decay in the neighborhood and greater motivation to see that things would get better. She felt that this could happen through active and powerful community organizations that could make business more responsive to the needs of the community and cause politicians to worry about their own futures.

During April of 1976 Fran began to feel run down. Her energy level was a little off. We attributed this to her busy schedule, possibly stress, and being overworked as she always devoted all of her energy to any project she undertook. But our friend Leah said, "I think you are pregnant." We didn't think that was possible as that was something we were not planning on and trying to avoid. After the condition was confirmed by Fran's doctor we had an important decision to make. Both of us were satisfied with our lives. Having a child was not something we thought about or discussed. We went away to the Bear Mountain Inn for a weekend to talk it out and decided that if we were to plan having a child it would never happen. This was an opportunity for us that we would never have come to on our own. Having a child is a major responsibility and if there is one way to describe us it is responsible, among other virtuous character descriptors. Bringing a human being into the world and having to care for it for at least 20 years would certainly change things for us but we were ready for the obligations it would present.

The way we approached having a baby, one would have

thought we were the first couple to do it. We took Lamaz classes and read many books on childbirth and child rearing. We had meetings with other expectant parents. In a way it was another project. We redid one of the parlor floor rooms for the baby's room. We borrowed a beautiful antique crib frame, purchased new bedding, recycled an old carriage and prepared the room. Freshly painted with varied colored circles on the walls and ceiling and string glued to the circles so you could mistake them for floating balloons.

And then we had a baby girl. Sarah was born October of 1976 into a loving and caring household. Working to make the environment safe for her and to offer enough space for freedom and exploration was challenging and worrisome. I learned many things during this period about relationships and how to relate a little better. I wasn't always successful but the effort and journey was worth it. A great book that I read at this time was "How to talk to kids so they listen and how to listen to kids so they talk." It was even relevant for adult communication, sometimes.

Fran was exhausted by the delivery but it only took a few days for her to redirect her energies to the child rearing as well as with all her other issues. It was also about this time that Fran came across an ad in The Phoenix, a neighborhood newspaper, for a 20 unit coop of summer bungalows that was being formed in the Catskills. Fran thought it would be great to have a summer place now that we had a child and she had fond memories of her own summers as a child in the Catskills. There were several meetings over the next couple of months with the founder of the coop and other people interested in buying into the coop. Fran found a lawyer and the group hired him to represent our interests. We very quickly became the owner of a 2-bedroom, with porch, summer bungalow that was modestly priced and didn't need much work to make it livable.

CHAPTER 9

In November 1976 there was a fire that destroyed the homes of the families living at 656 and 658 Carroll Street. This fire was believed to have started in the basement of one of the buildings and was determined to be caused by an electrical fault. But a fire was only one method among many that was used by unscrupulous landlords to force a building into vacancy. The block association organized a collection for those families left homeless, helping them get essential household items, clothing, linens, kitchen utensils, pots and pans and dishes, canned foods, furniture, as well as cash donations. The block association worked with Rev. Stephen Giordano, the pastor of the "Old First Reformed Church" at the corner of Carroll Street and 7th Avenue. The church became a collection point for donations. The pastor, noting that these same problems were faced by many families in Park Slope, and with the collaboration of the United Block Associations (UBA) of Park Slope, an organization that the Carroll Street Block Association was a member of, started a program to offer assistance to those affected by emergencies such as the fire. All donated items would be stored in the church and a schedule for receiving and distributing items was set up.

It was at this time that Fran read a study by the New York Public Interest Research Group detailing mortgage redlining that was occurring in Brooklyn. The study was titled: "Take the Money and Run: Redlining in Brooklyn." Several federal laws had been passed (the Home Mortgage Disclosure Act of 1975 and the Community Reinvestment Act of 1977) to make bank activity more transparent by requiring disclosure of the bank's investments and enabling organizations to petition government to redress problems. This enabled the research group to study mortgage activity and it was clear that Brooklyn was undergoing systematic and massive disinvestments. The study showed that racially integrated areas had fewer mortgages and Park Slope was not an exception. The study covered seven major Brooklyn savings banks and their mortgage practices and was reported in the Brooklyn Brownstone newspaper ("The Phoenix") by Marsha Reiss. The conclusions were that "...the banks are choking the flow of credit in Brooklyn." They reinvest "...only a tiny percentage of their Brooklyn deposits into the same Brooklyn communities that give them their wealth."

The banks listed in the study were Brooklyn's largest judged by assets. They were Brooklyn Savings, Metropolitan Savings, Dime Savings, East New York, Greater New York, Greenpoint Savings, and Williamsburg. Greenpoint's mortgage record was not criticized as they made 722 mortgage loans in Brooklyn worth $25 million while Greater New York only made 44 valued at $1.1 million. Several banks, Anchor Savings, Brooklyn Federal, Hamilton Federal and Independence all invested heavily in Brooklyn, indicating that it was still a good business practice and you could still make a profit by lending money in these neighborhoods. It was understood that if banks do not extend credit and make loans and reinvest their depositor's money into the neighborhoods where it came from for home purchases, home or business renovations, opening new businesses, and other related activities, growth would be stifled and decay occur.

Several socially conscious groups, including The United Block Associations of Park Slope (UBA), the United Methodist Church, The Fifth Avenue Committee, Pratt Center, NYPIRG and local residents met in January 1977 and took on the goal of making banks more responsive and to act responsibly in the communities where they obtained their deposits. Their goal was to make sure "that banks should reinvest a substantial amount of their deposits into the community they derived the deposits from." To achieve this reasonable business arrangement they undertook an education program for block associations in Park Slope, devised strategies to deal with the banks and politicians, and reach out to residents and merchants. They endorsed closing accounts and withdrawing funds from banks that do not invest in the communities where they obtain deposits. They strongly urged residents to support banks that lend money to residents of Park Slope even to the point of trying to encourage one bank to open a branch in our community.

At this time Tim O'Hanlon was hired to survey the member block associations of the UBA to determine their views on a number of issues including bank redlining. There were many people in the community who thought this issue important enough to confront the banks and started a new group, Against Investment Discrimination (AID). This movement was very effective at getting and involving people around the issue of "redlining." The bank that was selected as the target for action was The Greater New York. They had a major presence in Brooklyn as more than 90% of their deposits were made by Brooklyn's residents, yet gave fewer mortgages than any other bank. Groups were organized to challenge the bank by withdrawing funds, making deposits using coins, creating long lines to disrupt service, closing accounts, picketing, and anything else they could think of to be a nuisance to the bank.

Because of Fran's involvement in the community she became one of the strategy leaders of AID. Many meetings were held in our living room to come up with methods to make banks responsive to the communities where they received the bulk of their assets. The Greater New York became the focus of their actions. AID found other banks, who didn't want their names publicized, but would gladly accept new depositors. They even discussed having a bus available for people closing accounts at the Greater to be driven to the new bank, but that never occurred. Eventually, after meetings with the president of the Greater New York bank by several community groups, concessions were made, and a tenuous peace was formed. Upon the passage of the Community Reinvestment Act (CRA) which forced banks to do more for the neighborhoods they are supposed to serve, AID was disbanded.

Fran continued to attend community meetings, collecting data for her dissertation that included defining group problems that included aspects of organization structure, funding, community outreach, political activity, etc. Along the Fifth Avenue corridor there were several groups trying to address similar problems. The merchants groups were primarily concerned with crime and drug activity. Residents groups were similarly concerned with the drug and crime problems but there were other issues they formed around. Safety issues, housing abandonment, prostitution, low income tenants being gentrified out of their homes, home buyers unable to get mortgages, loans for home improvements were unavailable, and home insurance was difficult to obtain. As noted earlier the major financial institutions had written off and would not invest money in the neighborhood. In order to succeed these groups had to present a solid and unified front, which they did in 1976, when they combined forces to form the Fifth Avenue Neighborhood Committee. Through their diverse skills and interests they were able to bring pressure to bear on city agencies and state representatives to obtain help in addressing some of their problems.

By 1974 Fran had begun her dissertation. I am not sure what led her in this direction as the path was not a straight line for her. When we moved into Park Slope she became aware of the banks divestment policies and the difficulty in obtaining a mortgage. Growing up in the south she witnessed the burden that segregation placed on people. She would tell stories of her childhood and how she couldn't comprehend why black people who took care of the households and children of white families were never considered their equals. Fran's "nanny" cared for her in warmer ways than her mother did and Fran loved her. She couldn't understand the restrictions placed on her "nanny" as they were sometimes forced into separate spaces such as the back of a bus or in separate public bathrooms. I think her sense of justice is the bedrock of her personality. Her values were defined by her experiences and she recognized the injustice of redlining and how demoralizing it was. I don't know where her strength, obstinacy, and perseverance came from, but they were the qualities that made her as successful as she became.

Fran's dissertation studied an urban neighborhood, her neighborhood, Park Slope, and the people and organizations that were affected by housing policies, housing abandonment, displacement, crime, gentrification, bank and insurance disinvestments. The study covered 20 community organizations whose meetings she regularly attended. The dissertation is well written and shows intellectual clarity. She knew her topic, formulated her thoughts clearly and presented them in an easily readable and understandable form. It does not have the technical jargon that sometimes makes such work an effort to read and understand. It took her ten years to complete and in 1984 she received her doctorate.

Not being a person who would shrink from responsibility, Fran not only took notes of the meetings she attended, she also became an involved participant. She always liked, if possible, to control a situation and I am sure that she easily made her opinions known and gave advice wisely and freely at these meetings.

I am not being excessively complimentary when I describe Fran as a person having vision, courage, intellect, creativity and the ability to sell ideas. She was extremely altruistic as shown by all the volunteering she did and at times in leadership positions. She had a generous personality and magnetic charm that drew many people to her causes and generated friendships that were helpful in creating successful projects. One of these was the Fifth Avenue Committee (FAC). It was formed combining the groups that made up the Fifth Avenue Neighborhood Committee to become a more effective force for neighborhood change. At this time Fran was involved in collecting data for her dissertation, raising her daughter, running one of the most effective block associations in Park Slope, was president of a coop board for a summer bungalow colony, all amidst the rest of life's activities.

In the Park Slope community where there were many "chiefs" Fran became a major actor. When the FAC was incorporated in 1978 Fran was its first president. Geographically it encompassed Fifth Avenue from Flatbush Avenue to Prospect

Avenue, a distance of about one mile. The area was composed of three and four story buildings with residential housing and businesses intermixed. There was some abandonment. You can check her dissertation study for more details. FAC's purpose, as a not for profit organization, was "to promote the well being and betterment of the community. To discuss with members of the community common problems of urban dwelling. To assist and aid the community to promote commercial revitalization, a clean and safe environment, beautification in the community and other acts of things incidental to or connected with these purposes." FAC was very successful and the organization is thriving more than 30 years after Fran's involvement with it. I spoke with one of FAC's early employees, Rebecca Reich, who spoke admiringly of Fran's ability and leadership. Rebecca was hired with monies obtained from the city's "Comprehensive Employment Funds" that were distributed to reputable organization and then funneled down to the neighborhood level organizations. I am certain that Fran's knowledge of whom to contact was instrumental in obtaining these funds for FAC. Fran was able to obtain space on Fifth Avenue from Al Cabbad, a merchant who owned several properties in a run down area with abandoned buildings. While Fran was President the organization broke ground for a new supermarket in a neighborhood bereft of a store for grocery shopping, renovated houses on Warren Street and had new housing built with an effort to maintain reasonable market rates that ran the entire length of Baltic Street between Fourth and Fifth Avenues.

In 1998 the Fifth Avenue Committee had a 20th Anniversary Party celebrating the completion of 100 buildings and 500 units of affordable housing being renovated. They honored those who inspired and struggled to make the dreams of a safe and vibrant community come to fruition. Of Fran they said:

> She knew the challenges of trying to improve and redevelop a community like lower Park Slope while simultaneously preventing displacement and creating

opportunity for low and moderate-income residents. Those early strategy sessions and years of hard work laid the foundation for the next 20 years. Since 1986 she has been the executive director of Neighborhood Housing Services of NYC, a not-for-profit organization committed to preserving and revitalizing neighborhoods by financing and rehabilitating housing, providing education for low and moderate income people and developing grassroots leadership. She has become a national leader on homeownership and credit issues.

Fran, in response, said, "One of the most exciting and satisfying experiences as a neighborhood resident was founding the Fifth Avenue Committee and working with residents and colleagues like Pat Conway, Rebecca Reich, Gary Sloman, Annie Thompson, Frank Torres, and John Touhy to improve our community. The Fifth Avenue Committee is a premier organization that has made an enormous difference."

A wonderful attribute of Fran's was never taking all the credit for a successful project, event or activity. She would always be certain to mention the names of others who were less vocal but who also shared in the efforts. She was selfless this way and it made me very proud.

CHAPTER 10

When I met Fran I was working at Chase Manhattan Bank as a computer programmer. For the decade of the 70's I worked at five major firms, Chase Manhattan Bank, Manufacturers Hanover, The Federal Reserve Bank, Johnson & Higgins and Teachers Insurance. Large banking or insurance firms were the only organizations that realized the advantages of computerization and could afford it. To get ahead in this field, meaning a better salary and/or position, you just changed your resume by adding your most recent job description and changed your employer. Another reason to move along, and this was mine most of the time, was my inability to understand some of the decisions of management or to work within their requirements or idiosyncrasies. At times decisions were made for political reasons, at other times for personal advancement, at times not to appear incompetent or rock the boat and draw attention to yourself, or to cover one's ass. But then I could be wrong so let me offer two examples from the many I encountered.

At one firm I was hired as a senior analyst to design a computer system for a new department within a bank to manage and promote a factoring function. I was hired by two men in charge of the project who were "Senior VPs" and they had a budget of over $1 million dollars to implement the system. Not knowing anything about "factoring" I told them I would like to interview the members of the factoring team who could describe what they did and how they needed the data to be processed. It was difficult getting appointments with the staff, almost as if they were avoiding me, but I persevered and eventually had the information I needed to plan the system. The VP's sent me to several meetings with computer salespersons to find out what equipment was available and what support they would offer the project and I wrote up reports of these meetings. I did this work for five months. During this time there were two computer consultants who came in every day and sat at their desks doing nothing. I couldn't understand how they could do this day after day. They said that this is what they were being paid to do. When I was asked for a final review of the project and how to proceed I advised the VP's that the process they were trying to automate could really be managed with a micro computer and that they really didn't need high end mainframe computer equipment. I further expensed the project at about $80 thousand dollars. I was fired the next day.

One of the major projects at another firm was printing an annual investment statement for all of its customers. This project took almost a week of printing on very fast computers and high-speed printers. Most of the work was done at night but it impacted and delayed every other project of the computer department. The way it worked was that a large form, 14 by 20 inches, was created by a printing firm. This form had space for individualized customer information that was added to the form from the company's customer data base. After the job was completed someone noticed that there was an "i" on the form that had two dots above it. What to do? At a meeting I attended I tried to explain that everyone receiving the form only cares about the numbers that we extracted from the data base and probably wouldn't notice or care about a double dotted "i". But management did and they reran the job. By that time I had decided I would be better off as a computer consultant, working on my own.

The late 1970's were the early days of the microcomputer revolution. Drew Yskamp, a colleague, was at New York University, completing a Masters degree in computer science. He asked me to help him with the code for his thesis, a simple accounting system that he was designing to run on a Radio Shack microcomputer. We worked well together and I enjoyed coding the programs. The project introduced me to the world of microcomputing and I saw its potential for individuals, professionals, and small business. I decided to try and sell this system, set up systems, and train people who were interested in learning about computing. My first foray into consulting was a total failure and within a year I was back on Wall Street. With the help of contacts I had made I was able to connect with a labor union who needed support for a computer system they had purchased that was not working at all as they envisioned and an importer of glass products who wanted to computerize a manual system. This enabled me to leave the corporate environment and work on my own advising clients, setting up computer systems, training and supporting them as the field changed. It was a grand profession and worked well for me.

As the decade of the 80's began, Fran was busy on many fronts: working on her dissertation and attending the meetings of 20 neighborhood organizations, connected with a childcare collective, and making the Fifth Avenue Committee a force in the neighborhood.

She was also interested in our tiny, 12 x 24 feet, backyard garden, planning on what plants would go where based on color and height and when they bloomed and what vegetables to plant and in what order. Originally she mapped everything out on paper before executing the plan. Once the garden was well in place she discarded her maps. Her energy was boundless. Because she never enjoyed driving an automobile (I think her sense of direction was bad), on weekends she had me hooked as her assigned driver. I would drive her to pick up the garden supplies and then be her laborer to help in preparing the soil and the plantings. I really didn't mind as we were together and working on a project where we could share in the results.

And so the decade of the 70's came to a close. It was a good decade for us and to recap: we met, were committed to each other, married, purchased and moved into a three family building, our home, that we still live in, and raised our daughter. One of our tenants has been with us since 1974 and the other one since 1998.

Through the years with Sarah

CHAPTER 11

I am writing this part of the story on June 24, 2012, our wedding anniversary, 41 years to the day when Fran and I were made "legal." To celebrate, we are in Spring Glen, the bungalow community that we joined 36 years ago, and am having one of the days that have become our norm, meaning I will recall coming here but Fran won't. Fourteen years after being diagnosed with Parkinson's, Fran also has some dementia that limits her memory. We really don't talk to each other much anymore. She also eats half her meals with her fingers and is incontinent. But then I am getting ahead of myself. Where was I?

Oh yes, Fran was working on her dissertation and taking care of Sarah. That was much of what she was doing then and it kept her totally occupied. As for me, my consulting business kept me pretty busy as well. I would either be at a client site, trying to promote additional work, reading material to keep up with the ever evolving field of computing and managing stuff around the house. Fran was collecting information for her dissertation and putting it into written form using an IBM Selectric Typewriter. Whenever she had to make corrections to her papers, even minor ones, and to satisfy her committee advisers, she would have to retype entire chapters. She didn't take easily to a computer's word processor but eventually realized how efficient it was and how much easier it made correcting her manuscript. She had a fear of the machine and it took several months for her to get comfortable with starting it up and loading the word processing software and the document she was working on.

During the summer months of 1978 through 1983 she would go to our cabin with Sarah and her computer and work on her dissertation. Getting through the graduate program was not easy. It required persistence, intelligence of a sort, some people skills, diligence and the ability to change how you think, reorganize your thoughts and recognize what your advisors want to see and how to please them. Fran's paper was very different from what her department expected. It took her 10 years to complete the program but she finished it on her terms. Her paper on community change was accepted with the support of several academics who she was able to get on her thesis committee and that had progressive ideas and a background in community activism.

We also worked together to find a school for Sarah and we fell in love with The Woodward Park School, which had very progressive ideas about what an education for children should be, such as learning how to think and not just memorize. It was a wonderful and enriching environment for Sarah, and Fran and I were delighted and appreciative that our daughter experienced this.

Perhaps our ability to make decisions together which were satisfying to us both owed to our being different and brought diverse talents and strengths into the coupling. For those who know me, I don't spend too much time thinking deep thoughts. I'm a kind of superficial guy. Fran on the other hand was the deep thinker and organizer in our family. Our relationship was based on an 85/15 percent division of labor. I always found or made the time to help Fran with her projects. She was never too shy to ask for help or somehow work it out so that someone would ask her if she needed or wanted help. I, on the other hand, would generally do things on my own and not ask for help. For example, we bought our first car after Sarah was born and had purchased the summer cabin. I decided that I would do all my own repairs and maintenance for the car and I did. I purchased the manual from the manufacturer and the necessary tools and car ramps. I changed the oil, changed points and spark plugs, and re-gapped whatever needed gapping. Replaced brakes and brake drums and the muffler. Removed the engine head and reset the gaps on the points in the cylinders.

So I wonder, what are the forces that make a person become who they become? I'm from a family with three children.

My brother and sister and I are very different yet we were raised by the same loving parents, grew up in the same household, went to the same religious services, attended similar schools, yet we have become totally different persons. My siblings maintained their religious identity and continue practicing the rituals they were raised with. I no longer perform those rituals. We all have retained the good values our parents instilled in us and that has nothing to do with religious affiliation or training. Somewhere along life's path I veered off onto an unexpected direction. I have no explanation for why this happened. Something in the brain was wired differently or some chemical I inhaled. I don't know.

Fran is another example of someone working against the mold. By all accounts, and considering her early years, you wouldn't think she would become an example for what a human being should be. A broken family at childhood, a biased environment growing up, an unstable home environment, moving between schools, a mother having a nervous breakdown, a husband who beat her, and having to work while attempting to finish college at night. There was a lot to overcome.

Even in childhood her friends found her sincere and helpful. Her teachers thought she was a pleasant child. Was she compensating for her home life? Who knows? Her experiences hardened her but did not make her hard. They strengthened her but did not make her rigid. Somehow she incorporated these experiences, knowing how she wanted to be treated, into her persona for how she dealt with others. Her background and education helped her develop the values that she lived by. She felt that all people should be treated fairly, justly, equitably, and sympathetically. In January of 1985, expressing these views, she wrote:

> I know now that the relationship between the haves and the have-nots are inextricably intertwined. We know by now that New York City is becoming increasingly polarized and all around there are those with high paying

jobs, a little savings, who can afford a nice home. Taxes are down. Inflation is lower. Opportunities for the small investors have improved. I go, on fun, if simple, vacations to the Catskills. My neighborhood is well maintained. So why do I care? The question is why don't we care? We feel badly for the homeless when it's cold. Shake our heads over the terrible quality of education for some kids. Get angry at the increasing graffiti that defaces neighborhood institutions and parks. What we don't always see, is that an incidence of birth and of course the proverbial hard work that we were socialized to engage in. We are where we are and the poor, minority, uneducated and in some cases criminal are also there as an incidence of birth and culture. That's unfortunate we say but what has that to do with us? Everything.

When your fellow human being is poor, so are we. When people are pushed to the wall, some die quietly, others fight back, society judges them criminals. We become their victims. It is not only if we don't help people to change the system we will be victimized. It's that the implications of increased police and jails without increased opportunities have implications far worse. How do we identify these criminals, by the color of their skin, their language skills, their religion. What will be the first rules of apartheid and what techniques will be used to separate ourselves from "them"? How will we objectify and dehumanize others? It is very hard for us as individuals to identify the criminals as co-victims. Especially when we struggle ourselves and our leisure time is in front of the tube that fills us with soft mushy stereotypic good guys and bad, the same as our newspapers.

There was a goodness and altruism that encompassed all that Fran did. It was exhibited in her choice of dissertation topic, her work in the block association and her choice of civic organizations she joined. Even with her iffy background she was a risk taker. It might have been her sales background where she learned that not making the sale at this time was only a minor setback and to just try again until you accomplish your goal or it could have been her personality that allowed her to succeed in this area. I don't have the answer except to relate that succeed in life she did.

I remember two incidents that can help define her. How she would see a situation that she felt needed to be addressed. Would determine the risks and assess the possible outcome. Then act in a way that was creative and possibly have an alternate solution up her sleeve if the first route didn't work out.

The first incident was when Fran saw a woman abusing a child, who was being difficult, on a subway train. Fran, without apparent forethought, stood up and confronted the woman. Fran always thought that being an authority figure would lend credibility to whatever she was doing, and so she said:"Excuse me. I am a child psychologist and I couldn't help notice what was going on." Both the child and woman paused in their interaction to listen to what Fran was saying and their squabble ended.

She did the same when she saw a man mistreating a dog and was able to change that situation as well using a similar technique."Hi. Excuse me but I am a veterinarian and that is no way ....." Very creative.

I really can't explain what is going on cerebrally that makes people turn out to become who they eventually become. Just enjoy the journey, if it is a good one.

CHAPTER 12

Fran never wasted any time and was always busy. Working on her dissertation gave her a new direction in her life and her search for her own identity. She really took this seriously. The subjects covered in graduate school opened her to many new ideas. She became more politically aware and socially concerned. She took her writing endeavors very seriously and wrote on many topics. Her writing style depended on the topic, her audience, and was very personal and became polished. She could be humorous, or serious, or academic, or descriptive. But no matter what she was writing it was always stated clearly, in sentences that were just the right length. She also fashioned her writing so that it always would be interesting to whomever was reading it. This may have been because of her very strong sales background that was an important component of her personality. She was always working to keep "the customer interested and satisfied."

For over a decade, starting in 1973, she was presenting ideas and concepts to peers and professors by writing them down. The material would then be critiqued, possibly rethought and rewritten for approval. This process helped Fran improve her skills at putting ideas on paper clearly, analyzing problems and situations, understanding the questions to be addressed and proposing answers for a solution, seeing the minutia in the topic and having a grasp of the big picture.

Once she had gathered all of the data for her dissertation she pulled back from many of her other projects and devoted her time and energies, physical, mental, and psychological, to its completion. At this time Sarah was quite young and they would spend summers in the Catskills. I brought a computer up there for her to make it easier to continue her writing and to ensure the security of the material she wrote. She really enjoyed her summers with Sarah and they formed a wonderful mother/daughter bond.

After she had completed her dissertation she continued to write on other topics. She began a diary. Her thoughts were expressed in prose and poetry. She wrote expressively, cogently, and rhythmically and as I read much of the output, almost 30 years later, I find it enjoyable, entertaining, and moving. She was a talented writer who wrote in an interesting and entertaining way.

Take her diary. I don't know what qualities it takes to form a personality and why it varies from person to person. Is it the climate? Dry days as opposed to humid ones affecting the chemistry and neurons in our bodies and alter our experiences and how we perceive them? Does stress or comfort create new and different pathways in an individual? I don't know how these things come together to form a working personality but in Fran's case we have someone who was always open to new possibilities. She was like a sponge, absorbing new ideas and ideologies while she studied for her PhD. This didn't really bring her any comfort as she sought to find her place in the world. I know that sounds melodramatic, but Fran was that kind of a person. Although we never had long discussions about her philosophy of life, at the time she must have felt my quiet support, and that helped her move forward in her search for identity. What she wrote in her diary shows a thoughtful person having doubts, yet someone willing to explore topics and issues that were painful and full of risk. Anyway, I'll let you make your own insights, ending this chapter with two separate diary entries written by Fran in early January 1984.

1/3/84

What better way to start a diary. 1984, the year of big brother. All the thoughts, inspirations and magnificent obsessions that came to me over French toast and Tropicana are gone. Only the banalities of doing dishes and cleaning the rocking chair that I just moved to the living room from my study stir my conscious. I know it's because I am afraid I have nothing of interest to share. And so if cleaning house is all that I can concretize out of my fear, let me start there.

Over the holiday when Sarah and Moe have been home, I have cleaned house. Usually Moe does most of the cleaning. Not because he likes to clean but because he hates the animal hair balls that accumulate in all our corners. I don't like them either but Moe sweeps and damp mops them away. Then he brushes our dog Carroll and our cat Shoo-Shoo, trying to forestall the inevitable for a day or so. No, I cleaned because my cousins Stephen and his wife Shelly were coming to visit. I tried to disguise it as a regular cleaning operation. I don't know if Moe realized it, but I don't want Sarah to think people only clean when company is coming over. Moe always says we should clean for ourselves, and not for others.

Like my mother, I still clean mainly for others. Sometimes I think I could live like the Collier brothers, with newspaper tunnels all over the house and the smell of wet dog lingering on the paper as the poor "behema" tries to remember which tunnel has her food bowl in it. I think the poor "behema" is me also, overcome by piles of paper in my own house. I try to keep it under control and provide a good example for my child. I want her to know that mothers don't always work on papers and go to meetings but that sometimes they Windex glass, Fantastic banisters and change beds and towels. So I make it into little projects for us to do together and I feel smugly successful and most of all condescending to many of my friends who hire a weekly someone to help them lessen the load. I tried it once for a few months, but as soon as Sarah said "why do I have to do it. Let Mrs. Pierce do it." I stopped. You know, I think what I just wrote was a lie. I don't think Sarah ever said that at all. I think I just fabricated an excuse not to have to hire someone to help clean house. Why do I have to do that. For God's sake is it that I feel so out of control that I must have total control of the Windex.

I worry that if I don't keep cleaning, I will be overcome by filth and I won't care. Then what will everyone think of me. I shudder at the terrifying implications.

Dostoyevky shuddered at the conflicts he felt between a passionate hate of the moral ugliness of Russian peasantry and a respect for their stoicism and dignity. I shudder at the possibilities in store for me if I live out my fantasies of banal deviance from AJax. Am I a reflection of where we've come, or merely a drippy human being with superficial concerns or both? Or I hope and pray, am I being too hard on myself? After all, as a woman thrust into education, feminism and more rhetoric than my mother and I could clean in a lifetime, wouldn't one expect a little vestigial handy wipes swinging pink and yellow from our shoulder sockets.

Now I think I know one of the major weaknesses of my dissertation. It's too rooted in determinism. Trying to make every action ultimately understandable in terms of a political and economic historicism denies uniqueness of action. And yet it doesn't have to. As Irving Howe said about Frank's history of Dostoyevsky, historical placement doesn't diminish "our sense of Dostoyevsky's originality; on the contrary, it provides it with strong support." Why do I always tend to think that describing behavior within some broader context obliterates all that is original and explains all that is essential to understand. I never really understood Carl Popper's poverty of historicism thesis in graduate school but I knew we were supposed to reject him because we read him early in the semester and the truth always comes last.

In order to recognize my own originality, I have to, at some point, shed my total dependence on explanations of myself rooted in cultural, economic, political and historical determinism. I shall try to explore those ideas here, but I am very frightened. Suppose I find out I am a reactionary. I sound like one. I who tithe to social movements. I who reject the American Cancer society and instead bequeath my $15 to Linus Pauling and Vitamin C. I who have come to see racism and classism as a part of a unsupportable order and who pretend to understand George Gilder and fantasize about rejecting conservative doctrine while hoards of minorities, gays, and women cheer me on as I stand on a double tier of soap boxes (I'm only 5'1") in Times Square. This is probably my fondest fantasy. To my friends and for the sake of seeming normal, I try to pretend that it all wearies me, as I remember aloud (a euphemism for bragging) Tom Downy's recount of the Reagan war machine and how Air Force 1 will simply circle around in the sky the day after until all the radioactive particles settle down (like newlyweds in 31/2 room coops). Or having read Kurt Vonnegut's analogy likening those who build weapons to alcoholics (Nation, December 29, 1983). He imagines that they really don't want war any more than the man who drinks wants to find his head in the toilet of the men's room at Port Authority. While I nod at the imagery I feel so self righteous. My sloppy secret is that it doesn't all weary me, insufferable in others, and so right for me. I thought his last sentence was such a perfect ending for today, but in rereading I am nauseated and frightened at my protestations. I need my Moshe.

1/4/84
I'm never really satisfied. I spent most of the day work-

ing on my part time job as outreach committee chairperson of Sarah's school, Woodward. Last night I had a meeting with five other women from her school in the kitchen. It's a most peculiar situation. I feel comfortable in this job. It requires all the things I do well but hardly value at all. I organize the meetings, structure things so that we move along, people accept certain tasks directed at increasing enrollment in the school. Last year with my help the school got 20 new students, most of whom might not have come without my help. I enjoy the relationships between myself and the mainly women I work with. I do feel the job's important to the school, but I always feel this dull depression rather than elation when I've finished working on it. Today I drafted letters, recapped tasks, sent out notices, coordinated handing out invitations at a local school and spoke to numerous local papers and people about upcoming Woodward events. Is it that I'm bored? I can't figure it out.

I can't help but compare it to my other part time job teaching in the Urban Studies department at Queens College. Sometimes when I'm there earning my $1,500 per semester, I also feel a numbness of spirit. But more often than not I'm mildly titillated, not so much by the actual teaching, which is satisfying enough, but by the attention that is paid to me by the men on the faculty.

The faculty is comprised mainly of white men earning $40,000 to $50,000 as in most universities. There is only one full time woman, Alice, in health. That's where the women are, health and education. She's nice but not at all attractive and the other part time woman, who is the wife of the chairman of the department is totally off-the-wall. So that leaves me. Fortyish but attractive and smiling, always smiling. Last week under the pretext of seeing what a jock I am, one roly-poly pink-face professor felt my thigh to feel how hard it was. I even played the game by picking up my skirt ever so slightly. It's senseless to make jokes about who was harder. What was really hard was my inability not to play. It was as if I were programmed to respond to all professorial overtures with the appropriate aria. It never really went anywhere but I'm starting to have lunches with different tenured faculty members. I don't even see them as people with names but as professors with tenured fangs. The relationship is shaped by those things that never fail to separate men and women. When I first became friendly with roly-poly he immediately became paternal, arm around shoulder, let me take you to the faculty club friendly. There was never even a pretext at an equal collegial relationship. With Alice it was not like that at all. We've socialized, shared ideas, enjoyed each other's company. Yet I want to stay in, to play, to pity myself, to be self-contemptuous.

At Woodward it's all too easy. There's no status. Only the potential of wonderful relationships with other women and the knowledge that you've helped an educational institution that's worth something. Who cares about that? What can it buy you? So it is with all the middle-aged church going Italian women on my block who dealt bingo for the church on Tuesday nights for 15 or 20 years, who sorted cast off clothing into bundles for the poor, who manned untold fair booths all for the greater glory of God. Who cares? What do we win? For some, a shoulder shrugging eyebrow raising awareness that they did what they could. For others, a sense of bitterness at the emptiness of the cemetery trips to visit graves of husbands who left them calling numbers at the bingo instead of sunning in Miami. I want to love working for the school for the sake of the glory and inner good feelings. I need to be like that. Damn those professors and their capitalist appendages, those creators of values, those deciders of what I'm worth, what I like, what I am, and what is worthy of status and high pay.

Suddenly I feel tired. Have I figured out why I don't love my Woodward work? I hope not.

CHAPTER 13

Fran was teaching at Queens College as an adjunct professor while she was completing her dissertation. She found the experience very disappointing. She didn't enjoy the academic environment nor the fact that she ended up correcting the spelling and grammar of student papers rather than the content. She was disturbed by the salary paid to adjunct professors and thought it was tantamount to servitude. She was upset that female professors took a back seat to male counterparts. She did not like the commute. Traveling to the college by public transit could take several hours and although driving there by car was shorter, usually less than an hour, she never liked driving on city streets and highways. It always made her nervous.

One of her students informed her of a job that was opening in the Brooklyn neighborhood of Kensington/Windsor Terrace. She told Fran that she thought she would be perfect for the job of Executive Director at the Neighborhood Housing Services (NHS) office which was a Division of NHS of New York City. Somehow she knew that Fran would be ideally suited to and enjoy the work. I don't believe Fran knew what the position would entail but it was a chance to get out of the academic environment that she did not enjoy and she would not have to deal with the long travel times that she hated. Fran interviewed for the position and was immediately hired. I don't think there were many other candidates for the position but even so, she must have wowed the board with her energy and vitality, charmed them with her personality, and overwhelmed them with her credentials. Winning people over was one of her strongest skills. All she had to do now was understand the mission of the organization, learn its procedures and guidelines, follow through with the details and not let anyone down.

The NHS office was about two miles from our home and

in good weather she would walk, through Prospect Park, to work. The job itself fit her personality perfectly. NHS is a not-for-profit organization committed to preserving and revitalizing neighborhoods by financing the rehabilitation of housing stock, providing education for low and moderate income people in credit distressed communities, and developing grassroots leadership to foster self sufficiency in these neighborhoods. She would be the decision maker, the visionary, the gentle authority figure. This was a role she relished and excelled in. Of course she had to answer to a board of directors made up of community residents but she was able to work with them and impress them with her dedication, responsibility, work ethic, reliability, and honesty.

Managing the board was the easiest part of her new job. The executive director she was replacing had planned to leave the organization for the better part of a year and hadn't devoted much attention to the day to day administrative needs. The office was in a four room, second floor apartment. It needed some repairs and changes to make it the kind of place that Fran would want to come to and feel comfortable in. She had a staff of two; an administrative assistant and a construction manager. You should know another thing about Fran: she never gets discouraged. She just gets to work.

This was Fran's introduction to the NHS model of neighborhood revitalization. NHS programs were supported by a national umbrella organization that provided training and some financial assistance for neighborhood organizations to function and succeed in their mission. The neighborhood group was formed in communities within a low to moderate income census tract. The model was to have a board made up of community residents, business owners, bankers, and politicos who had an interest in improving the neighborhood. Through outreach programs, NHS would find residents whose homes needed repairs and offer to help with the project. They would determine the cost of the repairs, put together a proposal, get the financing approved, find an approved contractor, and supervise the job to completion. That is what NHS did and that is what the NHS offices around the nation do. Fran loved the job.

She wasn't pleased with the situation in her office when she found out that the financial books had not been maintained and that the financials were in disarray. She wasn't overjoyed with the physical layout in her office and its appearance. She was not familiar with the computer that she found on her desk and this caused her some concern. No big deal! Within a short period of time she had things humming smoothly.

She hired a bookkeeper to make the books sound. She made the office space more people friendly by rearranging furniture, repairing fixtures, painting walls, etc. She wanted to make the space livable for staff and presentable to clients, vendors, supporters and anyone who visited. She learned an entirely new business model, from scratch, by reading everything that came before her. This was a new project for her and she was excited by the challenge. She grew more confident and stronger as she learned what the organization was all about and what was required of her. The skills she brought to the job helped her in working with her board, staff, and others individuals who were involved with the organization, from neighborhood residents and vendors to politicians and contractors. This was another challenge and all that was needed was understanding it, analyzing methods for solving the problems, and applying a solution. Does that sound too simple? I believe that is how Fran functioned. Every problem can be solved, somehow, by the lessons her academic studies had taught, logic and cooperation among the parties.

She loved working at NHS because she was able to help people fix, repair, and remodel their homes thereby bringing happiness and feelings of success into their lives. She brought people together in a common goal of helping each other and improving their neighborhood. The organization became a success because it was well managed. Projects were initiated, supporting documents maintained, financial ledgers balanced, contractor bids reviewed, construction monitored, and signed off at completion by the NHS office. Fran found the process very satisfying. With her strong organizational skills she had the office and its projects moving along with ease and satisfaction for all concerned parties. It was a success and she loved it. I think this was the happiest time in her life.

I am not stating the case too strongly. When Fran formed a relationship she would give it her all. She loved the people she worked with and they loved her. I have seen how people, employees and colleagues, responded to her in a positive way. With respect for what she did and how she did it, and for her commitment. She also bonded with the people she worked with in a way that made their jobs more meaningful, filled their effort with purpose, and made project completion satisfying. There was a magnetism, a force about her, which drew people to her and created strong bonds and a desire to accomplish goals. But for Fran, even though there was no time to rest as there was always another problem to solve, another person to help, another donor to interest, she was more relaxed with herself, enjoyed what she was doing, satisfied and never seemed to stop smiling.

CHAPTER 14

When Fran joined NHS, the agency had six divisions (branch offices) in New York City's five boroughs, all of them helping residents with housing issues. Being part of the national "NeighborWorks" organization they all had the same mission, similar organizational structure and tactics in raising funds. There was also a central office in Manhattan, NHS of NYC, whose job it was to coordinate with the branch offices in helping to raise funds and training of the staff as well as a bunch of other stuff that "main offices" do: attempt to set standards, help the branch offices with problems, provide guidance, offer training, resolve board issues, etc, as well as raise funds for its own needs. But there was a major structural problem as each neighborhood office felt they were independent institutions. In each neighborhood they rented their own space, they elected their own boards, raised funds from their neighborhood businesses, had their own computer systems, found their own customers in their communities, and completed construction projects. They didn't think they needed the NHS of NYC to give them advice or supervise their activities. This was a major problem with and flaw in the NHS corporate structure.

Each NHS division felt very distinct and distant from the NHS of NYC. They were in poor underserved neighborhoods in the boroughs while this "main office" was in Manhattan. They competed with the "main office" to raise funds from the same institutions. The divisions didn't think the NYC office understood what they did and that they really didn't need assistance except when they wanted it and would ask for it.

In 1986 the Executive Director of the NHS of NYC had handed in his resignation. Upon hearing this Fran decided to apply for the job feeling confident that she could do the job as well as anyone else could and that her experience in the Kensington/Windsor Terrace office had provided her with an understanding of what the job entailed broadly and in detail. She was certain and confident that she had the administrative and management tools, and the necessary people skills for the job so she felt no qualms in applying for the position.

Fran got the job (I'm sure you guessed that was going to happen.) But you might not know that when she took over the office was falling apart. The problem was a bad business model. An unwieldy corporate structure that pitted the borough divisions against the "main office." Fran had stepped into a very difficult situation. She was hired by the board, or so it seemed, so they would have a person in charge when the organization would close its doors. They thought the problems were insurmountable. They didn't realize that Fran was not a quitter and does not know how to concede when there is something that she wants. (I have seen her swallow Scrabble tiles at the end of a game so that she didn't have to deduct points from her score. Only kidding.) I will say that she felt quite satisfied when she was hired for the position and saw it as a sign that she was coming along in life, advancing and making her mark, achieving more than she had ever expressed to me about any career desires. And then the significance of the problems hit home and she became worried but never despondent or depressed.

At the time Fran took on her new position there were less than 20 people on staff. Two divisions in the Bronx had to be closed due to malfeasance, theft of equipment and people on the payrolls who never showed up in the office. There is something you have to know about Fran. She is very thoughtful about how she spends her money or money that she is responsible for. On two successive Saturdays therefore, she enlisted the aid of some staff and friends to help her remove all of the papers and documents related to the financial and rehab work of the Bronx offices. She had a sense of responsibility and felt she could be held accountable for their failures. She also removed all office supplies and equipment that we could carry, typewriters, computers, printers, adding machines, etc, etc, etc. I know because I was one of the people she enlisted to help her. Once again she had to hire a bookkeeper to put the NHS of NYC accounting records into a reasonable order. These were difficult days for Fran and somehow, I am sure, they prepared her and made her strong and gave her direction for what she would accomplish later on.

Her task was to take an organization that was floundering and considered to be on shaky ground and ready to declare that it was going to close its doors and turn its prospects around and make it a success. Really! That's what she saw confronting her. Whether she did not want to be seen as a failure or felt that what she and the organization were doing was worth saving, she started being Fran.

This was the beginning of a 17-year journey that transformed Fran and the people she met on that journey. No one that she met was untouched by her humanity, ability, desire, humor, intellect, charm… wow, I am getting carried away and you probably think I am being biased. But this is what a colleague, Elaine Dovas, says about Fran:

> I think and am inspired by her energy, her fearlessness, her willing to take a risk. I remain in awe of how she retains her sense of self in all situations. Of the con stancy with which she interacts with others: Fran treats CEO and homeless equally.
>
> Fran has a cool mind that rationally seeks to find what decision makers need and provides for that need so as to accomplish her political and programmatic objectives.
>
> Fran has an intensity and focused drive coupled with her assertive nature she will take the ball to the end, oblivious to all else.
>
> Fran has vision and is charismatically able to communicate and seek to bring others to her vision.

Sometimes I lose energy. Sometimes I give up believing in my ability to obtain goals, meet objectives. Sometimes I think why daydream? It cannot change a situation. And I then when I think of Fran's forceful determined nature, I am renewed and resolved to try again.

See, I wasn't kidding. To write about Fran's impact on people and her accomplishments at NHS would require a book of its own, but I will try to encapsulate these achievements as best I can. As I noted, when Fran arrived as the Executive Director of the NHS of NYC in 1986 there were 20 people on staff. When she left they were employing more than 100 people. The financials were in a mess when she started and when she retired in December 2003 the accounting department employed a dozen people to maintain the records that had grown into a complicated automated fund management system. The entire office was computerized and networked. When she started there were six branch offices and she had to close down two of them within weeks of starting the job. When she left there were nine locations. When she arrived the annual budget was $800,000 and the loan portfolio of the same amount, $800,000. When she left the annual budget was $9,000,000 with investments in neighborhoods throughout New York City of almost $200,000,000. When she started they were a neighborhood group making neighborhood change with local support. When she departed they had national recognition and impact.

Fran was able to take this not-for-profit corporation that was at risk of closing its doors and give it new life beyond her wildest thoughts about success. To accomplish this she actually devoted her life and well being to what she considered a very meaningful vocation. Helping people secure and maintain their homes and communities. She brought tremendous joy and happiness into the lives of people who had not given up hope that they could have their own home. She realized that if she could make NHS of NYC into a viable organization she could help many more people and families in low to moderate income neighborhoods. To do this she worked tirelessly, creatively, altruistically, intelligently, maintaining relationships, and by being able to work with a broad strata of persons at different social levels.

What do I mean by tirelessly? Well Fran worked a seven day work week. If she left the office early in the evenings it was to attend meetings. Otherwise she always worked late and would bring work home. On weekends, if she didn't go into her office she would work at home. Her greatest wish at this time was that she wouldn't have to sleep as much as she did so she could get more work done.

What do I mean creatively? Fran was dedicated to helping people. It was a calling for her and to succeed NHS needed private and corporate funding. To introduce funders to the work they were doing she organized bus trips to NHS neighborhoods so the funders could see for themselves the impact their contributions would have on the lives of people. She would take them into the homes to meet the people that NHS served and helped. Nothing like a happy satisfied customer telling you how much they loved NHS and how they couldn't have fulfilled the American dream of home ownership without them to make the sale.

Steve Alschuler, successful in public relations, writes this about Fran:

> This may sound strange, but Fran has had a significant influence on my life in ways I'm just beginning to realize. I always admired the fact that, even when presented with more lucrative opportunities, she made the choice to devote her life to work that served other people. As I've been contemplating my own future and considering certain possibilities, I've often asked myself: What would Fran Justa think of my doing this or that? Would Fran think I was living a good life, spending my time in the right way?

> I was thinking about Fran just last night in connection

with an organization I've become involved in that runs an after school program for kids in a bad neighborhood. Last night, there was a fundraiser and I was designated to get up and make the pitch for people to write checks. I channeled Fran who, of course, could indeed get blood from a stone, and I'm told I did a pretty good job. Afterwards, I pictured Fran coming over, patting me on the shoulder, telling me I'd done a good thing - then telling me to get off my butt and do more.

What do I mean altruistically? Fran was always helping people. It wasn't only on the job. Her ethical and moral base was founded on treating people honestly and fairly. On the job her sense of responsibility to her customer base, her funders, her staff, the neighborhood boards, was truly incomparable. She kept her salary at a reasonable level to her staff when compared with other not for profit Executive Directors. Earning a larger salary did not excite her as much as accomplishing "good things."

Susan Draper, a neighbor, remembers how thoughtful and supportive she was:

Although I have always known of Fran's important civic community and political work, beginning with the 5th Avenue Committee and then her not-for-profit housing business, what I remember most about Fran is her acts of kindness. When we first moved to Carroll Street, over thirty years ago, a small fish store on the corner of Garfield & 5th Ave, was going out of business. Fran went up and down the block asking (more like pleading) with people to go buy fish from this mom & pop store so that they wouldn't lose everything.

A few years later I had a miscarriage. This would have been Michael and mine's first child. Fran just took my hand and went shopping with me, consoling me with her presence. Fran was always able to combine intense activism with deep and abiding concern for people, for the people for whom she worked tirelessly.

What do I mean intelligently? Well Fran was quite the intellect. She met with bank officers and CEO's and enticed them to become involved and fund NHS projects. She had on her board leaders of the banking and insurance industry and government regulators. She taught at Neighborwork's training sessions around the country. She wrote articles relating to housing topics in industry journals, magazines and newspapers. Every year she was a speaker at many events.

Doug Dylla, a colleague, writes of her:

Fran has had a huge impact on many of us in the NeighborWorks network. She is a leader, a mentor, a sage, a friend, someone we respect, love and admire. While I had know Fran for years earlier, it was probably her work on the NeighborWorks Campaign for Homeownership that really took our relationship to a whole new level. Fran really provided visionary thinking in that national collaborative effort that helped us move the whole network to a completely different relationship with each other, with our partners and put us on a very different national stage.

Her clarity of thought and clever ability to develop "brandable names" such as "Full-Cycle Lending" helped align everyone in the network around a common vision and attracted many new partners and resources.

Time and time again in meetings and brainstorming sessions, Fran was able to describe an exciting idea about some remarkable future outcome. While it often seemed unreachable or unattainable at the time, the more we discussed it, the more real the goal became. And more often then not, if we adopted that goal, we seemed to reach it or even surpass it. To me, it became clear that it was the vision, the creativity, the goal setting that was a critical part of the planning process and Fran was truly a genius at that work.

And yet, when she offered these ideas, it was in very gentle ways with lots of humor and respect for others. She was a consummate practitioner of the "servant as leader" philosophy. She was always ready to help out on projects, to listen to others, to share ideas with anyone, and to help anyone that needed it.

I have learned much from Fran and am glad to share these few stories with others to recognize her genius, her creativity, her lifetime of hard work, her leadership and her overall generosity of spirit. Thank you, Fran!

What do I mean, maintaining relationships? She knew how to connect with people for she was caring and sincere and it was that part of the interpersonal dynamic that people loved and respected her for. She kept a data base of all the people her business was involved with and knew their spouses and children's names, their secretary's name and if she could get it their birth dates. Even the names of their pets and when she would speak with them she would get personal because she really cared about these relationships.

John Aloisio remembers her well:

Fran was the kind of person that one can write not just a book, but volumes of her many talents, accomplishments and wonderful things she did for the disadvantaged through her years at Neighborhood Housing Services.

Among my responsibilities at Sterling National Bank was

Community service and investment so that is how I got to know Fran so well. Sterling is a committed community lender but only a fraction of the size of the New York major banks. But that did not stop Fran from asking us for ever larger and larger financial grants to NHS. I eventually had to explain that we did not have those kind of giant budgets but that she could count on us to meet many of the smaller needs that over time would add up. Well you can guess, and I learned well about Fran, when every month we were asked to make a grant after grant to buy a new computer, or fax machine, or copier. After a while, I lost track of the sum total of our little grants but they were probably not that small in total.

That was Fran personified. But she was also the kind of person who then selected Sterling Bank for one of NHS's coveted annual recognition awards, not an easy thing for her to pass over all of the other large bank officers present for the event. I was called to the stand, commended for our Bank's support and given a certificate and the microphone. I stood with the microphone in total silence for a moment as most of the audience appeared to be rather surprised at the recipient. To break the silence, I will paraphrase my brief remark:

"Well, I guess this is as close as I will ever get to an Oscar so I will start by thanking my mother and father, but most importantly I would like to thank Fran Justa for making it impossible for me, for all of us here, not to want to support NHS. Thank you Fran."

The laughter and applause for Fran and NHS was overwhelming. For me, it was one of the most memorable moments of my long banking career. I missed Fran since retirement but I will cherish knowing her because the life she lived only deserves celebration and joy.....joy for the lives of the many people who were fortunate enough to come to her attention and care.

And did I mention my wife was persistent. That is why Fran was a fabulous fundraiser. Many people thought her success was due to her fantastic ability at getting individuals who controlled the purse strings of corporations to be generous. Fran, however, bristled at this claim to fame. She preferred to think of herself as an organizer, a thinker and mover, a generator of ideas, able to make dreams come true. Susan Safire, a colleague says:

I had some fundraising experience before I joined the staff at Neighborhood Housing Services, and although I was mentored by one of the best fundraiser around, nothing compared to what I learned from my true mentor Fran Justa. Who else in this world would be able to get the top, and I mean the very top, CEO's to sit on the board of this small (at the time) not-for-profit. Here was an organization that at the time only had a budget of $1.5 million and yet Dick Parsons, CEO of one of the biggest corporations in America said "yes" to Fran.

But that is not all I remember so fondly of when it came to Fran. I can remember the two of us leaving a meeting that we had with the head of a bank, decompressing over a cup of coffee afterwards, and discussing tactics. I also remember us ditching going back to the office after a meeting and going to the baths downtown for massages. What fun times we had.

And I'll also never forget the day we were walking on, I believe it was 5th Avenue, and a homeless man was sitting on the floor next to a building with a sign asking for help. Fran dug into her purse and gave him $10. I said, "Fran, $10? Why so much" and all she said was "Why not".That was Fran and the type of person she is. Dr. Justa is smart, funny, emotional, full of life and truly in love with her one and only Moe.

Forgive me, but I had to leave that last comment in.

CHAPTER 15

I want to talk more about Fran's many accomplishments, so many successes and victories on behalf of neighborhoods and communities in New York City and beyond. From 1986 to 2003, Fran recognized problems that should be addressed, and with vision and skill helped develop solutions while building and managing a strong and vibrant organization. This is excerpted from her bio:

• Management of corporate operating budget and loan funds totaling $45 million.

• Management and planning responsibilities include marketing and publicizing existing programs, new program development and implementation, board and committee development, corporate, government and regulatory relations.

• Co-chaired and helped to develop a National Homeownership Campaign to target low-income borrowers through the Neighborhood Reinvestment network.

• Developed Full Cycle Lending concept designed to ensure credit quality and provide maximum neighborhood impact through consumer homebuyer education, appropriate lending products, inspection services through consumer education - home maintenance training programs and early intervention delinquency counseling.

• Developed the First Homeownership Center in the Neighborhood Reinvestment network. Subsequently Congress provided Neighborhood Reinvestment with $25 million to fund Homeownership Centers throughout the country.

• Developed consumer homeownership counseling programs and clubs in Brooklyn, the Bronx, Queens and Staten Island to help low-income renters prepare for ownership.

• Developed Latino consumer homeownership program to reach Spanish-speaking renters.

• Developed research proposal to uncover barriers to housing lending in immigrant communities and initiated new NHS program in immigrant community.

• Created multi-family and mixed-use consumer rehabilitation lending program for buildings fewer than 20 units, and emergency loan programs for 1-4 unit buildings.

• Increased funding base from 34 contributors to 220.

• Computerized financial and fundraising management systems.

• Developed consumer Financial Literacy Program and curricula.

• Developed a Research and Planning Department to measure the impact of NHS services on the lives of community residents.

• Developed a Section-8 Homeownership Program where low-income renters can eventually move into homeownership.

• Developed the New York Housing Guarantee Fund after the tragic events of September 11th to assist those affected who either lived or worked in the Ground Zero area.

Fran and Dick Parsons, 1995 at the NHS Gala

Fran accepting the NHSEF Neighborhood Vision Award, June 1996

With President Clinton at the National Homeownership Ceremony, 1995

Fran and Hillary Clinton at the National Housing Conference, 2003

Fran with Tom O'Brien at the 2003 Gala

Although Fran achieved many of her goals throughout her career she never stopped to rest on her laurels or brag about her success. She would say "The world is not a perfect place and there was always more to do to repair it."

I really don't know how to present her most productive years while making it believable. I know she was energetic, tireless, a superstar in her field, honored during her career in many ways and in many forums. For example, in 1990 she was honored by the Brooklyn Borough President as one of the outstanding women of Brooklyn. And in 2003, The New York Housing Conference and The National Housing Conference had its 30th Annual Awards Dinner attended by more than 1,450 professionals in the real estate, banking, insurance, investment banking, development, architecture, law, government and advocacy sectors. The keynote Speaker was Hillary Rodham Clinton. Fran received the "Lifetime Achievement Award" and was introduced by Dick Parsons, the CEO of Time Warner Corporation, who said:

It is an enormous honor to have been asked to make this introduction. Fran is more than an old and dear friend, she is someone for whom I have the utmost admiration and respect.

In my new line of work, in the media and entertainment world, we have an expression one uses when referring to great accomplishments over an extended period of time. We call that, a "body of work."

When Fran joined NHS in 1986 as Executive Director it had a staff of 20 people. It had an annual budget of approximately $800,000 and a loan portfolio of approximately the same size—$800,000.

Today NHS has a staff of over 100, an annual budget of $9 million and investment in neighborhoods throughout the City of almost $200 million. In 1995, Fran created the first NHS sponsored Home Loan Center in the entire nation. Today there are 65 of these throughout the country, making it possible for tens of thousands of low income citizens to become first-time home owners.

In 1996, Fran conceived of the Full Cycle lending concept, a system that brings together lenders, non-profits and government to ensure that low income people can not only gain access to credit to buy a home, but that teaches them about home ownership and prepares them to be owners, thereby reducing the risk of delinquency and foreclosure down the road. Today, NHS has educated over 14,000 people through this program.

You see my point. This is a women who, through her body of work, has changed the face of this country.

As I thought about what I might say that best summarizes for me what Fran is all about, I remembered something Dr. Martin Luther King, Jr. once wrote while imprisoned in Birmingham, Alabama during the great movement. "Injustice anywhere is a threat to justice everywhere. We are caught in an inescapable network of mutuality, tied in a single garment of destiny. Whatever affects one directly, affect all indirectly."

Fran Justa understands this better than anyone I know, and her life has been a reflection of this understanding. For all that she has done to make this City and this world a more just place, she is most deserving of the honor being bestowed upon her this afternoon.

High praise indeed. But there is more. In 2003, Fran was one of a select group of respected individuals in the community development field to attend a special seminar at the John F. Kennedy School Of Government at Harvard University, "Achieving Excellence In Community Development." And in 2001/02, she received the James A. Johnson Community Fellows Program of the Fannie Mae Foundation award. This was a stipend for one year to pursue any interest she was interested in. During that year she would provide The Foundation with quarterly reports on her topic which was succession planning in the not-for-profit organization.

Fran was also expert at getting publicity for NHS and its work and spreading the word about its offerings to the people and communities that needed it most. As such, she started a quarterly NHS newsletter that provided information on renovation loans, maintenance classes, landlord and financial fitness classes, home maintenance training, and classes preparing one for a home purchase. In addition, Fran was interviewed and quoted in many publications and wrote many articles that appeared in newspapers, trade journals, and literary magazines. Here's a few:

- 1985 article in "City Limits" on Neighborhood Organizing

- 1988 article "Banking On Housing:The Income/Cost Conflict" that appeared in "City Limits Magazine"

- 1988 report to the "Kings County Democratic Party" for their Platform Hearings

- 1990 "New York Newsday" Brooklyn Profile person

- 1990 article in the "Daily News" Real Estate section

- 1990 article in "New York Newsday's" New York Forum section

- 1990 article in the "Village Voice"

- 1990 she appeared as the "Brooklyn Profile" person in "New York Newsday"

- 1993 "American Banker" article on reaching new ethnic groups

- 1994 article in "Neighborhood Reinvestment Corporation" magazine

- 1994 article in "Crain's New York Business" noting lack of insurance offices in urban areas

- 1994 article in "Neighborhood Reinvestment Corporation" publication on "Full Cycle Lending" program

- 1994 in "The New York Times" on subsidized single-family housing

- 1997 "Home Works" article in "The New York Times"

- 1997 "Daily News" selection for Brooklyn People column

- 1997 a discussion between bankers and nonprofit executives discussing the Community Reinvestment Act in "US-Banker"

- 1998 discussion in "American Banker" on an assessment of HUD

- 1998 "Storeworks" article in The "New York Times"

- 1999 article in the "National Mortgage News" on credit improvement loans

- 1998 article in "Caribbean Life" on awards presented to community children

- 1999 article in the "National Mortgage News" announcing a $2.5 million grant

- 2001 A "Queens Tribune" article on New York State funding for NHS of Queens rehabilitation and construction loans

- 2001 article in the "Brooklyn Eagle" honoring 20 lawyers doing pro bono work for NHS

Fran also found time to extend her influence in the community by becoming involved in many areas of the housing movement and active on the boards of many private and public corporations, including: Affordable Housing Advisory Council for the Federal Home Loan Bank; Atlantic Bank Board of Directors; Chase Manhattan Bank's Consumer Advisory Board; Community Capital Bank Advisory Board; Association of Neighborhood Housing Development; Board of Advisors for the New York Housing Policy Resources Project of the Community Training and Resource Center; Fannie Mae's Housing Impact Advisory Board Council; Federal Reserve Board of Governors Consumer Advisory Council; Fleet Boston Bank Community Oversight Committee; Flushing Savings Bank Board of Directors; JPMorgan Consumer Advisory Board; National Insurance Task Force; Neighborhood Reinvestment Corporation Campaign for Homeownership; New York State Banking Board; and the Women in Housing and Finance.

CHAPTER 16

Now I can look back at the time when we were in our thirties (the decade of the 70's) and think we did okay. We made some good decisions and were carving our own paths with some success. Our careers had direction and goals and we had a home in a neighborhood that suited us. When in our forties (the decade of the 80's) we continued to be active in our community, had a comfortable home, had a lovely daughter who seemed to be growing up nicely, were working at jobs that were satisfying. And when we were in our fifties (the decade of the 90's) things remained pretty much the same. Fran was as busy as ever but my life began to change. My consulting work didn't take up all of my time so there was room for house work, cooking, cleaning, shopping, seeing to Sarah's needs, etc. When Fran had meetings that were scheduled for several days in cities close by, such as Boston, Philadelphia, Albany, etc., I would drive her there. That way we could spend time together on the drive and at meals. Fran wrote this lovely poem to me, December of 1993, to show her love and understanding.

Ode to a Husband of 22 Years

When you pulled my arm straight up in the shower this morning as if you were trying to get to all the spots as you washed me, I knew you were trying to help me stretch.

When you held the dryer on my hair just the right distance from my head so it wasn't too hot, yet dried my hair just right, it wasn't a gesture, you stayed there until it was done.

When you watched me dance with a smile of appreciation and then you danced with me, letting me fall to the ground, doing dips and laughing with me, your arms gave me strength as well as the apparent joy we shared.

When you burst into the little meeting Sarah and I were having to write her application for Cornell to share the fact that Michael Feldman's phone system got screwed up and people from all over the country were on the radio phone lines, your sense of incredulity and laughter from deep inside of you was so contagious that Sarah and I caught it and we shook with laughter with you.

And all this joy was shared before noon today.

At that time I had a lot of freedom, could make my own schedules, take on only clients that interested me, kept up with the ever changing field of computers, and started taking trumpet lessons. I always wanted to play a musical instrument. Then early in 1997 my father was diagnosed with dementia and was placed in a nursing home. At the same time my mother was hospitalized with heart problems and when she was released from the hospital she moved in with my sister. I would visit my father two or three times a week, usually after he had his lunch. Then I would take him to the nursing home's cafeteria where I would have my lunch and we would talk, or rather I would talk to him. Sometimes he would recognize me immediately and sometimes it would take half an hour and sometimes he wouldn't recognize me at all. When he didn't recognize me he wouldn't talk to me. He would just glare at me and I know he didn't trust me then. Whenever we went to the cafeteria I would buy him a chocolate bar. On those days that he didn't recognize me he wouldn't eat the candy. I understood that he wasn't the same man he used to be and did not pressure him to live up to those older standards. My mother and sister would visit him and try and see him as he was in the past. They would ask him questions to test his memory. I saw his confusion and frustration when they would do this and never enjoyed my visit when they were there. On some Sundays Fran and Sarah would come along and we would visit him together. I remember him enjoying the company. He was my father. He was having a tough time.

I would also visit my mother every other week. Mentally, she was alert and fine. Her problem was physical. I had trouble realizing how ill she was as she was cognizant and you could have a reasonable conversation with her. But her physical abilities were limited. She had no energy and did not enjoy exerting herself. I would ask her to take a walk with me but she didn't want to be bothered. She tired easily and I am sorry I did not recognize that.

Visiting with my parents caused me to cut back on my consulting business. But that was okay as being with my parents made me feel better and I know that my father enjoyed my visits, when he recognized me. My father died on March 25, 1998.

That winter my friend Joe was diagnosed with cancer. His illness and the treatment were very debilitating and weakened him. He wasn't in the mood for visitors very often but we did manage to get together whenever he would let that happen. I never saw him at his weakest and his death on March 9, 1999 came as a surprise to me. Now when I think of him I still miss him and feel a warmth and love and friendship that doesn't disappear. I still am angry with him for never stopping smoking cigarettes.

My mother continued to weaken and died on March 24, 1999. One year to the day after my father's death. Roll it back to the early 90's. Carl Boger, Steve Dobkin, Phil Miller, Irwin Natov, and myself would meet for breakfast nearly every Friday morning at the Grecian Corner diner. Every once in a while one of our other friends would join us. After the Grecian Corner closed we continued the tradition at the Purity diner. Carl got cancer around 1996 but then the illness went into remission. Carl was so weakened that he couldn't continue his contracting and carpentry profession. At the insistence of his father in law and wife he began to learn, and succeeded at making quality violins. He was really into the art and purchased special woods and tools for his new avocation. He now had more spare time and we began to spend some of it together. Quite a smart and talented man that Carl, and I was very comfortable in his company. But the cancer didn't give up. It struck again in mid 1999 and Carl, weakened by the chemotherapy, could not continue doing what he really enjoyed. I made myself available to him whenever he had the energy. We would go for a walk in the park, go to a museum, or just hang out. Carl died on June 24, 2000 at the age of 52.

Looking back at these years you would think I should have been more aware to the fact that the people I loved were dying. I never recognized that. Maybe I'm just thick. It was almost like a passing thought. They were here and then they weren't. I didn't dwell on the dying part but I did feel the loss. It didn't immobilize me and I don't know if it changed me. I sometimes think these deaths should have had a stronger impact on me. Then I think not. When I think of my parents I am a bit sorrowful but I feel a sense of calm in the memory of those two wonderful people. When I think of my friends there is a mix of gladness that I knew them, anger that they are not here now, and loss that I won't see them again.

CHAPTER 17

During the 1990's Fran was at the top of her game. Every year was better than the last. NHS was doing more community outreach and investment. She was raising more money from funders. Her reputation drew private sector bankers, developers, contractors, and other leaders in the professional world to the ranks of NHS supporters. Each year NHS had a gala dinner event that would usually honor a major figure in either banking or government. This event was the major fund raiser for the organization and would fill a room for 1,000 people not only growing financially but having its reputation grow as well. Fran was a respected partner for projects she was involved in and NHS was trusted to accomplish the goals they set out to do and reported honestly to the funders on the results.

At the NHS gala dinner event on October 22, 2012, nine years after Fran had retired, Mark Jahr, the head of NYC's Housing Development Corporation, received an award named for her. In his remarks he lauded Fran for the work she had done.

It's a great honor to receive this award, and to be introduced this evening by my wonderful friends and colleagues, Mat Wambua and Bill Traylor. And it is perhaps an even greater honor to share this evening with Mayor Dinkins. Mayor Bloomberg's New Housing Marketplace Plan rests in part on the legacy of Mayor Dinkins' efforts, which, among his many initiatives like "Safe Streets, Safe City", laid the foundation for the revival of the City's neighborhoods and the City as a whole.

I'm also deeply honored to receive an award named after Fran Justa. When Fran was the Executive Director of Neighborhood Housing Services of New York City, she was one of those imposing Community Development divas, the equivalent of Patti LaBelle. In fact, she was a whole binder unto herself.

When I was at LISC, Fran would call me and begin singing her fundraising aria. No one sang it better. And I'd laugh and say "Fran, I should be sitting at your throne learning from you. You don't need me, I need you."

But beyond and underlying her audacity, her grand audacity, was her equally grand commitment to the neighborhoods and residents of this City—to the folks living in East Flatbush, and Williamsbridge/Olinville/ Wakefield, and Jamaica, and West Brighton, to all the neighborhoods that make up this great city. That's what empowered her to be so bold and relentless and righteous in her pitches. And it's that life long engagement, her enduring commitment to building this city's communities and a more civil society that makes this honor so meaningful and fraught, because what comes with it is not simply the aura of Fran's immense spirit, what comes with it is an obligation to act in a manner that honors Fran's commitment and values. I will try to do that. Thank you.

It was in December of 1997 that things began to change and that Fran began to have problems. Memory is a strange phenomenon. I look back at my life, at our life together, and it seems so misty and hazy. Like looking through a fog or window with a lot of condensation on it. Trying to form what is true and what I recognize as actual from what either is incoherent, something I remember incompletely, or never happened. As I look back in time I can't remember when we became aware of Fran's illness or symptoms. It is at times like this that I am sorry that I didn't keep a diary or journal. The only record I have of the time passing is saved tax returns.

As I was gathering "stuff" for this book I came across a spiral bound notebook that Fran starting making entries in starting on December 29, 1997. She labeled the first page "The Parkinson Trek." The entries run from 1997 through May 2003. Some of the entries are one liners noting how she is feeling or what she did that day. Others are several lines long, usually written while on vacation or a business trip, also describing her symptoms and some of the activities of the day. On December 29, 1997 the entry reads:

> Today Moe and I went to see Dr. Belok, a neurologist. He said I have Parkinson disease. The stiffness, the tremors, the micrographics, as well as the loss of balance and blank look. He had me stand and he pushed me backward and forward. The way I took little steps made him feel "Ah ha", and he seemed excited by the discovery. He told me to get a second opinion. That night we told SaSa (that is Sarah) together.

I guess we must have discussed Fran's symptoms prior to visiting the doctor. But I don't remember any discussions. From that day on I must have been in a fog, never realizing the severity of the disease we were facing. I seem to have been very reactive to all that would and did occur. That isn't completely true, but looking back and relying on memory, that's how I feel having to live with the disease on a daily basis. Fran kept good notes for a while. She was still working and did what Fran would always do: try and be organized, collect the data, try to make calculated and correct decisions.

On December 30th she wrote, "I never knew Parkinson's was related to micrographics. I felt sorry for myself all day. I tried to laugh. Did an okay job."

The journal doesn't contain daily entries. Fran would write what she felt were meaningful thoughts describing her physical condition and some activities of her day. On January 12, 1998 she wrote, "I feel better when I work. Very depressed and teary in quiet moments. Stressed because I keep loosing my balance.

Not dizzy but more comfortable shuffling. B vitamin diminished shaking. Thought about dying yesterday. Not for long. My daughter is beautiful and my husband such a joy."

But despite her struggles, it was difficult by just looking at her to see she had an illness. The symptoms were invisible, but she was highly aware of the changes in her mind and body, which she noted in her diary. For example, in January of 1998 we vacationed in Naples, Florida. Fran, in her diary, more like a journal, notes the places we visited and some of the people we saw, but also her symptoms, such as "more relaxed, tremor in legs infrequent, mostly when cold, cold easily, some stiffness, feel relaxed." And "Hung out on beach took 2 walks, worked 4 hours. B/L/D (stands for breakfast/lunch/dinner) in room. Relaxed, some tremors." What should be noted here is that she brought work along with her on vacation. Nothing could stop her. During one three day span, she spent hours writing up employee reviews. Each day she would complete three of them and fax them to her office in the City. This is the way Fran plans her vacations. Work a lot, some play. During these days she notes in her diary, "hand tremors" "tremors, legs" "stiff", and she underlined "very stressed".

They call Parkinson's a progressive disease. Now that is the most inappropriate descriptor you can think of. Progress is something that moves to a better place. It indicates that things will improve with understanding or time. But Parkinson's is none of those things. It is a degenerative disease and is always making the person that has it feel worse, uncomfortable, and sicker. Parkinson's is like an acid that is constantly wearing away at the "normal" human condition. It never gets better. It never improves. It weakens you and those who care for you. It robs you of energy. No matter what anyone tells you it changes a life for the worse. You can only realize that every day you live is the best it is going to be.

Starting in February of 1998 our lives changed, but not dramatically. At some level Parkinson's had snuck into our lives, dug and hole and made itself at home. We had to live with it. Every symptom had to be examined, tested, reviewed, analyzed, understood, and hoped to overcome. Early that month Fran carefully listed her symptoms as 1) loss of appetite and weight, 2) very tired and weak, 3) tremors, left leg (especially when cold) and foot cramps, 4) pain in left arm and shoulder also pins and needles, 5) arthritis pain in hand, 7) loss of balance sometimes, 8) change in handwriting to very small, 9) sudden memory loss more frequent, 10) cramps in left foot and hand, can't walk fast, 11) stiffness in body on left side, 12) confusion, loss of direction, 13) tremors worse when cold, and 14) bladder infection.

Looking for answers she quickly made appointments over the next several months with doctors having different specialties. I guess she wanted to find and identify the problem and understand what was happening. Maybe to cure oneself. She saw an internist for a colonoscopy, had breast mammograms, saw two neurologists, a gynecologist, dermatologist, had a bone density test, blood work reviewed, had a brain MRI for encephalitis, took an EEG, saw a urologist about incontinence.

For the next two and a half years Fran catalogued her ailments and doctors visits and lab tests and prescribed drugs and their effects and the books she read about Parkinson's. She noted if she had no pain or little pain or bad pain in her foot or in her calf or in her leg or in her arm or in her neck or back or a head ache. She noted if she had a problem with balance or not or if she felt tired/exhausted or not or was stiff or not or had problems writing or felt rigidity in her body or not. She listed the pills she was taking, both prescription and over the counter, and the times she took them and noted any change that the medications effected. She tried doing exercises daily that were recommended for people with disease.

Her notes were not only limited to her symptoms. She also listed meetings she had and the people she met, the Saturdays and Sundays she went into the office to work, business trips to different cities and her role, staff retreats and one liners about her conclusions, visiting my mother in the hospital, backyard barbeques with friends, shopping for a new wardrobe at the "Galleria Mall," work in the garden.

Although there were good days when she felt "normal" it was increasingly clear that Fran was having more and more trouble. On August 19, 1998, she bravely wrote in her diary, "Good day but I'll never feel good again. Hard to accept."

No two days were the same. Working became "difficult and overwhelming" when she had a bad day with "tremors inside that no one can see." I was told by someone who had Parkinson's that it feels like being a prisoner in your own body. "Not being able to move your body as you are telling your brain to do." Fran's speaking voice became softer and her stool harder, she was constipated. It was sometime around late summer 1999 that she records people telling her or me that she looks "really sick" and that she "moves slowly or stiffly and has a blank stare." She learned how to control her drugs, somewhat, so that she could manage her symptoms.

CHAPTER 18

From this time on we had this unwanted guest, an intruder, living with us. There was no way we were going to rid ourselves of this scourge known as Parkinson's Disease, which from now on I'll call PD, it can not be cured and there is really no way to slow its progression. In May of 2000 Fran stops entering daily information in her journal. From then until September of that year she only makes six entries and her last entries are "Exhaustion repeats, slowdown, job too much, first PD fall on subway stairs going to meet Mark Willis."

PD is like an unwanted house guest you can't get rid of. At first you don't notice anything odd occurring. But slowly, very slowly, bad things happen. You notice that money you left lying on the cupboard is missing. Over a period of time a spoon, a knife, a fork go missing. Then another place setting with dishes. Did you misplace your wristwatch? After a while you notice the table and chairs are gone and eventually the whole house disappears. That is how PD does its dirty deed.

At first PD doesn't make itself too obvious. There are simple complaints that seem almost normal or standard occurrences in life. Some cramping in the legs or feet while sleeping. I would massage them, when Fran mentioned it, until she felt better. Writing very small or speaking softer than normal, but with some concentration she could control that. Then she would be off to work. Fran was always off to work. PD could slow her down, maybe, but couldn't stop her. If you were to see her schedule and the activities she was involved with over the next five years you would not see any diminution in output. She continued to be active in all kinds of projects, committees, and forums through 2007. So it was possible to forget, at times, that she was ill and it was going to become more difficult.

Most of the time I didn't have a clue as to what the PD was doing to her. She would only complain to me when she was in pain. If she felt fine she would spend that time away from home, usually at work. How can I describe my annoyance with her at those times. When she felt fine she wasn't around. When she didn't feel well she came to me for support or help. Looking back I always helped her in those times of need. She could always call on me and even though I would help her I must have been annoyed and exasperated. In fact I know I was because as I think back over the past several years I am aware that we didn't get along as well as I would have liked or we could have if I hadn't been so upset.

Let me try and encapsulate all that Fran accomplished from the time she found out that she had PD, December 1997, until she could no longer function at an acceptable level for herself, sometime around 2007. I know this might seem humanly impossible for a well person to do and even superhuman for someone just diagnosed with PD, but this is some of what she was involved in.

Fran was really brave and continued working as hard as ever, or so it seemed to me. When she found out she had PD she began to plan for a successor at NHS who would be able to carry on what she had grown and developed. She read articles, actually did a study to figure out the best method to find and hire a successor. She met with her board and spoke with the CEO's of major corporations for their ideas. Eventually she did find a competent individual to replace herself.

On May 16, 2002 she was selected to be part of a pilot class for Neighborhood Reinvestment's Achieving Excellence Series with Harvard University. The class met for three days, three times over a one year period for intensive community development discussions that required preparation in various topic areas.

From early 2004 through 2007 Fran wanted to know how effective the Neighborworks Organizations homeownership education programs had been for low and moderate income household homebuyers as she felt this program, that she promoted, was an important tool for them. She raised over

$300,000 from the people and contacts where she had formed relationships with while working at NHS. The money raised was for the "Housing Environments Research Group" at the Center for Human Environments / CUNYGraduate Center to conduct a national survey. Surveys were returned by 759 households that were served by 13 not-for-profit counseling agencies across the U.S., thus yielding a unique database for examining the home buying and homeownership experiences of this population. This research provided a snapshot of how homeownership education affects a client's ability to buy a home, the financial and other consequences of homeownership, and the challenges buyers face after purchase."

NHS received a large portion of its working capital from banking institutions. As far back as 1995 she was aware of the threat to her organization by bank mergers as it limited her funding sources. She was prescient in this knowledge as noted in articles she wrote or was interviewed for in 2005 in the "American Banker," "Multinational Monitor," and "Shelterforce." She predicted problems to the economy and her lending base from the consolidation and predatory lending practices then occurring.

During July of 2004 Fran was appointed to the Board of Directors of New York State Banking Department by Governor Pataki. She was released from the board when Governor Spitzer took office in 2006. She then enlisted, primarily the support of Dick Parsons, to intercede for her reappointment which she did receive. She resigned from this board June of 2007 noting her reason as, "I now find myself in a position where my commitments are somewhat greater than I can manage comfortably."

Starting in 2001, several years after Fran was diagnosed with PD, she had copies of all of the emails she received at her office sent to her home computer. When I decided to write this story I began to look at her files and review the documents that were on her computer from about 2001 through 2007. I was stunned by the quality of her work. The clarity of thought and expression is evidenced in the letters she wrote, the articles she authored, and the correspondence to members of her staff, colleagues, business associates, discussing strategies and the needs and the ebb and flow of her corporation. She ran a tight ship. She had three to-do-lists that contained the same information but was organized in different ways so she had control of the important details from several vantage points. These lists were constantly updated as new items appeared and others removed upon completion. Her contact lists were organized in a similar fashion so she could maintain her relationships by name or company or affiliation with NHS. I really hadn't known Fran in this capacity. I now knew more about her skills and accomplishments and was very proud of her. She had taken an organization on the edge of collapse and made into a respected and functioning entity. She was recognized as someone who was creative, energetic and intelligent. She could make things happen.

CHAPTER 19

Parkinson's is a strange disease. Most people think it is a physical illness that causes people to have the shakes, professionals call it tremors, in their extremities. Or it causes one to have a blank stare or drool a bit. But at first you really don't see the effects of PD. It moves ever so slowly and it never stops progressing. I hate that word, progressing, to describe what is happening. PD affects the muscles, all of them eventually. PD is caused when dopamine is not being produced in the brain at a level that makes muscle action function easily and is only noticed when the brain produces less than 80% of what is considered normal.

Back in 1997, Fran had a minor bladder problem, the urge to relieve herself frequently. I believe this was the first symptom indicating she had PD. We went to a urologist and he said she had a normal problem for a women of her age and that it could be controlled with drugs. Fran began to take the medicine he prescribed and although it controlled the problem the side effects were unpleasant tiredness and dry mouth. At the same time she noticed a tremor in her left leg while sitting on the toilet. It must have been going on for some time because it prompted her to see a neurologist in December of 1997, who thought it might be PD and advised her to get a second opinion, which she did. That doctor also diagnosed the symptoms as PD and immediately wrote out three prescriptions. That's what doctors do. Write prescriptions. But Fran didn't fill them as she wasn't feeling well due to the bladder medicine and she saw no reason to take additional drugs that might have other unpleasant side effects.

Two months later we returned to the urologist to discuss Fran's reaction to the medicine. Fran told the doctor about the side effects and asked the doctor, "How long will I have to take this medicine?" The doctor responded, "For the rest of your life."

That was not acceptable to Fran and she decided not to take the medicine after that. As we were leaving the doctor's office and passing through the waiting room we noticed a book titled "The Best Doctors In New York City." Had to believe that. We found the name of a neurologist, Dr. Richard Lechtenberg, whose office was not far from where we lived and had our first appointment with him on April 20, 1998. This started our journey of doctor's visits that seemed to occupy us to distraction.

At our first visit Fran presented him with a list of complaints. Among the items on her list was that she had a tremor primarily in her left hand, a dull pain in her left shoulder for over two years (that we had attributed to strain from her carrying very heavy bags of paper work from and to her office and meetings), writing so small it was illegible, cramping in her toes, fatigue, lose of weight, and "stress incontinence" for about four years.

At the first exam Dr. Lechtenberg performed a battery of tests to determine the extent of her PD and described her condition as "very mild Parkinsonism" that was noticeable in "occasional mask-like facies and decreased blink." He also advised that she not take any dietary supplements for a month and he would have her blood tested to check for other things that might cause Parkinson like symptoms. He set Fran up with several appointments for an MRI and EEG to test other possible causes for her symptoms.

He did not prescribe any medicine until a month later at our second visit and then only a low dosage of Eldepryl which is a not too strong Parkinson medicine and is used early on in the disease. We really liked Dr. Lechtenberg as he was very cautious in his diagnosis and prescriptions and said he was not an advocate of new medications. He would only prescribe medicines that had been on the market for over ten years and had not been shown to have adverse affects. He would write up a report on each visit, give us a copy and send a copy to our primary physician.

On June 6, 1998 he wrote in his report "...on Eldepry 15 mg

bid and is moving very well. She feels better and reports that she is having less gait instability. She is more animated and agile and her gait is largely normal. My impression is she has well controlled Parkinson's disease."

Fran continued as a patient of Dr. Lechtenberg through the middle of 2007. Over that period of time her medication regimen changed as her illness required other medicines or different dosages to control her symptoms. She used more than eight different drugs during this period. Sometimes the medicines caused side effects that were so unpleasant that Fran wouldn't take them. Some of the side effects that Fran encountered were visions or hallucinations, dry mouth, depression, anxiety, confusion, and difficulty with memory. But, throughout this period of time Fran was well aware of what was happening to her body and the impact and effect the medicines were having on her abilities. She could talk to her physicians and explain exactly what was occurring when she took her drugs and her physical and emotional condition with or without them. She could make decisions for herself on whether or not to continue with a medication. The drugs that were being used were always being evaluated as they were very powerful and their impact on brain function or muscle control were not always predictable.

Towards the end of this period, sometime around 2007, Fran began to exhibit some strange behaviors. I am not sure whether to attribute them to her illness or her medications. She had a compulsion to buy more medicines and vitamins or supplements than she needed at a time. She would tell her neurologist that she was taking a drug four times a day when she was only taking it three times a day. She would never buy just one container of a vitamin or supplement. She would buy them three at a time. She was actually hoarding what she considered essential to her well being and she was frightened that she would run out of them and not be able to replace them. I didn't understand her being so irrational. I thought I was talking to her reasonably when I said, "Fran, you have been getting prescriptions whenever you need them. The prescription allows for four refills. We have never had a problem getting the meds you need. We don't even have to go to the doctor. We can just call it in to the pharmacy. Don't you understand we have everything under control and you don't have to worry?" But she didn't. She was adamant about what she was doing and couldn't hear what I was saying. She stocked her multiple bottles of medicines and vitamins and supplements in our kitchen cabinet. It took up an enormous amount of space for "pill" sized items. I didn't understand what was happening.

CHAPTER 20

The first seven or so years of the 2000's weren't really terrible. We knew Fran had an illness but it didn't impact our lives very much. It was more a nuisance than crippling. It did not force us to change our lives very much to either manage or deal with it, yet. Fran was still very active and productive, as noted earlier. She was successful in finding her successor. She was instrumental in getting funding for and taking a leadership role in setting up a national survey of Neighborworks organizations' clients to determine the effectiveness of homeowner education. The study lasted three years and was carried out by the Center for Human Environments at the CUNY Graduate Center. She was on several boards and committees.

Knowing that she would stop going into her office she decided to create an office in our home. We talked about her needs and wants and ended up building her a bookcase that was seven and one half feet high, six and one half feet wide, and nine and one half inches deep. It included a desk top that was four feet wide by two and a half feet deep and supported on one side by the bookcase and on the other by a two drawer legal size filing cabinet. I ran a phone line for her, set up a computer, installed some wiring for lighting and a cork board for pining up important information. The shelves provided her with almost 40 feet of storage space. The first thing she did was move books that she had saved from her graduate school days onto this bookcase. It was easy to utilize the rest of the space as Fran made copies of everything and even brought several boxes of paper work from her office that she deemed important. She brought folders that contained the 18 annual fund raising events that NHS had sponsored and that she had been instrumental in setting up. The folders contained seating arrangements, journals, invitee lists, copies of speeches, agendas, menus, etc., etc. Fran was detail oriented and her saving all these documents was a symptom of her illness and became problematic. She no longer had to leave the house to go to work but she needed help with her filing, organizing material, keeping lists and indexes of information, downloading and writing her emails so she hired an assistant who came in one day a week. I thought it was a good idea that she hired someone to help her and didn't realize that she did this because she was aware of the limitations that the Parkinson's was causing for her. Her desire to always work eventually became burdensome and created friction between us. But that occurred later.

At the beginning her illness did change our lives but in ways that were not easily discernible. Rick Roberto, the President of the Neighborhood Housing Services Board, remembers how she could still manage situations and people.

> Neighborhood Reinvestment Corporation (now Neighborworks) had a conference in Chicago. Fran and I attended the conference. I had never been to Chicago before and Fran suggested that we take the subway to our hotel, The Palmer House which was located at 17 East Monroe Street. We got off at the recommended station but did not see an exit for Monroe Street. We were in the middle of a large platform and didn't know which exit to take. Fran saw a police officer and asked him which exit was closer to Monroe Street. The policeman didn't reply because he had his gun out and was pointing at a young man as another police officer was in the process of handcuffing the young man. Fran asked him again and he said "Can't you see I'm busy". Fran responded by saying "Just tell me which way to go". The officer smiled (I think it was a smile) and pointed his gun in one direction. Fran thanked him and we went on our way. Fran's passion and dedication got the job done and changed people lives.

Fran also continued working in our garden. She loved planning where the plants would go, planting them, weeding to protect them, and arranged them so she could enjoy the display of colors and different blooms and sizes of the plants at different times of the season. Maybe she used this as a distraction to ease the stress of her job and now from thinking about the PD. She bought supplies and made sure the plants were watered on schedule. The garden was her baby. She would try to work early in the day before it would get too hot and she didn't lose her sense of humor, even when working physically hard.

Our neighbor Michael Goldberger remembers watching her doing her thing. "Several years ago, on a hot summer day, I was in my yard, just two down from Fran and Moe's. I looked over, and Fran was working hard in the garden, dripping wet with sweat. I told her she looked hot. Without missing a beat, she replied 'Twenty years ago, I would have taken that differently.'"

The people who met her at this time and knew she was ill were impressed by her energy, as was Dee Yalowitz, a friend from one of her support groups who remembers going to Fran's office just before she retired and how vibrant she was. And she was vibrant, creative and innovative, and her mind was always chugging along. Her PD didn't seem to stop her. Somehow she pulled herself away from her work and we went on week long summer hikes, in California and British Columbia, with the Sierra Club. How did Fran prepare for these hikes? Well we didn't pack too much as we weren't going to need any formal attire. I was carrying all the baggage so I had some say into what to bring along. Fran, however, was determined that we should bring our "oldies song sheets." When I was a teenager I had typed the popular songs of the day that I heard on the radio and over the years had placed them in a binder. It was fun to break them out every so often and have a sing-a-long. Fran thought that the people on the Sierra Club hikes would love to sing these songs as much as we did, and she was right. She made a dozen copies to hand out. She knew her audience. Back at the lodge and after dinner we would break out the song sheets and everyone joined in to sing. It was a great way for the group to bond and it improved everyone's outlook and certainly helped with the group's camaraderie.

Fran did take office work with her on these trips but after getting up early in the morning, having a lumberjack's breakfast, hiking along mountain trails, having a large supper and then spending the evening singing songs with our fellow Sierra Club hikers, she had no energy for working. She managed quite well on our hikes. The pace was gentle as were the slopes. I walked along beside her keeping an eye on her in case she needed assistance. I remember these times as being a lot of fun and relaxing for both of us. We shared in an adventure. Nothing could be better.

In the spring of 2001 we were sitting on our stoop with some of our neighbors and mentioning that our 30th wedding anniversary was coming up. Our friend Lisa Kaiser asked if we had any plans as this was a big one. We told her "No, we really don't have any plans. Maybe we'll go out to dinner with some friends, or something."

Lisa said, "You've got to do something! This is a very important event. A milestone." Lisa was into parties. She is an artist who works for a production company and she began to tell us what we had to do. "Have a big party and invite all your friends. Have some great music and food. And you must do a sing-a-long of your favorite tunes. You guys love to sing and do it well. What are some of your favorites? List them so you can have the sing-a-long."

So we sat on the stoop and discussed how to set up this anniversary party. We came up with a list of songs to sing and rented the hall at our temple for about 130 friends and neighbors. We had a great jazz trio, a dj, and the food was all pot luck. People love pot lucks. People prepare the best of foods and our friends Frank and Jill Friedman almost always make franks and beans that they prepare to perfection and it is about the only time I ever eat them. At each table seat we placed our song sheets with about 12 songs. We told everybody that this would be a sing-a-long of some of our favorite tunes and we were sure they would know them. At first there seemed some reticence as people looked around the room to see who would start singing but after the first song everyone joined in and sang with abandon. It was a fabulously unforgettable evening that everyone enjoyed.

We also spent one week for two summers at a jazz camp in Maine. I play the trumpet and wanted to go the camp where I knew several of the musicians. Fran did not play an instrument but she came along so we would be together. When we arrived at the camp, Christine Correa, who managed the camp, took Fran under her wing and taught her some bluesy torch songs, "Summertime" and "Cry Me A River". At the end of each week there was a recital at which Fran was in her element. She had a great voice, could sing, and loved being on a stage in front of an audience. She brought the house down.

Sierra Club hike, 2000

Sierra Club sing-along

Nova Scotia, 2007

CHAPTER 21

I said earlier that these past seven years, from around 1998 to 2006, weren't really terrible. Fran's illness didn't impact our lives very much. It was more a nuisance than crippling. It did not force us to change our lives very much to either manage or deal with the illness, yet. I don't want you to think that all was roses and sweets. We continued doing the things we normally did but had to add some new activities because of the PD. Fran did her thing by doing research and trying to find out more about her illness. She would contact PD organizations. Compile a list of reading material. Read several books written by physicians who said they could cure or slow down the progression of the disease. She bought into this concept and began to order "supplements for the brain" that came in jars. She was going to take charge of this, whatever "this" was, and control it.

People who have PD, it seems, are always looking for something that will rid them of the curse that they live with. They continually hope for a solution, a cure, a remedy, something that will bring normalcy back into their lives. We would see our neurologist every 6 to 8 weeks. He charted the progression of the illness based on Fran's description of her ailments that did change over time but remained under control because of the drugs that were prescribed and the fact that PD is a slow moving disease. The complaints during this period were fairly consistent but varied in intensity. And then some would disappear and then reappear from time to time or give way to other symptoms. Balancing the drug intake against the PD problems sometimes caused their own difficulties as the drugs themselves could cause a variety of physical and mental abnormalities.

Over this period Fran noticed a problem with the gait of her left foot and at times this would cause her to misstep and occasionally fall. She was having trouble sleeping and would be fatigued much of the time. She had visual delusions that were caused by her medication. She would see insects or stationary objects moving or a mouse run across the floor. The doctor noted in May, 2002, "she has good control of her Parkinson's disease, but her recent acknowledgement that she is having visual delusions is worrisome and will undoubtedly require changes to her medication regimen in the near future, if they persist." Fran decided to continue with the medication because it made her feel more energetic. She felt she could manage the visual delusions/hallucinations because she understood it was the medication that brought them on. Fighting the Parkinson symptoms and managing the medicines became a continuing balancing act.

I went with her whenever she went to see her neurologist. I did this as much to be with her and support her, and maybe, although I wasn't aware of it at the time, concern for her condition. Fran also started attending monthly support groups. The first, early on in her illness and around 2001, was at Beth Israel Hospital and was named the "Young Onset Parkinson's" group for people who acquire the disease before they are 60 years of age. She would go to the meetings, which started at 6 P.M., directly from work through 2003 and after that from the CUNY Graduate Center where she was coauthoring the housing survey. I always would meet her there and it was here that we saw the toll that the disease had on people. The people who attended the meeting, there were usually from 15 to 25 people, were mobile, many exhibited tremors, dyskinesia, stiffness, facial masking, and freezing. Several managed with walkers or canes. All had some incontinence and there was always a rush to the bathrooms before and after the meetings.

Fran did not approve of the way the Beth Israel meeting was being run. She wanted the meetings to have structure and goals and after three meetings she was considered the group's leader by those who attended and they looked to her for inspiration and advice. She created an agenda that had everybody introducing themselves at the beginning of the meeting and discussing their complaints and medications. People seemed very attentive at this part of the meeting and held on to every word about medication and would ask each other questions. This was the most active part of the meetings and took up most of the time. After that either a guest speaker or the R.N. who hosted the meeting would discuss current issues in the Parkinson community. Everyone was attentive, it seemed, hoping that something would be said that would be miraculous and healing. But most disturbing and depressing with this group was that each individual must have known that there is no cure and the symptoms would only get worse.

The socializing aspect of the group was as important as the instructive parts. At the end of each meeting a song was sung and without a doubt everyone loved this part, sang loud and happily. Fran then suggested that the group go out for dinner and usually about six people would do so. She made these meetings a social event and it became more interesting for those who showed up.

After several years her interest in this group began to wane. She no longer was working in Manhattan and going to this support group in Manhattan was inconvenient. She found out about the Brooklyn Parkinson's Group that met weekly at the Mark Morris Dance Studio for movement and singing classes. There she met Olie Westheimer who organized the group and was its steady and firm motivating force. Fran inspired Olie to be persistent and not be afraid or doubt herself when she needed something to make her dreams or ideas a reality. She says of Fran:

I did not know Fran well. But she helped me and BPG (The Brooklyn Parkinson's Group) too. First thing, she was so active and energetic. She exercised so much and with such enthusiasm. And she was very flexible; maybe from working with those huge balls she showed us one day. We had one in the dance studio.

Our first singing leader did not work out, he was won-

derful but too academic for people. And I don't think
the leader was happy either, Fran suggested to me, "ask
William." He'd be great." I said, "I can't do that," he is
hired by Mark Morris and he does not seem interested.
Fran kept insisting. And she was right of course, because
of the music William loves. So I asked him. He agreed.
These days, we have 30 to 35 people in singing class.
William has become a part of BPG.

After several years Fran joined two other groups. One composed only of women who had Parkinson's and the second for
women who were "in transition." Women facing life changing
situations who wanted to share their experiences and have support. Fran participated in these groups for several years and
when she no longer was comfortable riding the subways I
would drive her to these meetings, bring something to read,
and then wait for the meeting to end and drive her home. We
did this until she no longer could, sometime in 2009.

CHAPTER 22

Those were the good years considering what was ahead for us. It seems Fran's memory, her abilities, and skills, were beginning to falter and although she was aware of this, I was not. Not that I am so thick but I was not tuned in to how Fran was functioning. I had lived with her for over 30 years and she was always capable, competent, talented, alert, vivacious, and etc., etc. That is the woman I knew. She had been completely in control for years while managing a complex business and having loads of responsibility. I didn't recognize that things were changing right in front of me, every day, because it was so out of character from that which I had known. It took me a long while to understand what was happening to my wife and it was a difficult time for both of us.

I think her medication was altering her personality and causing her to become difficult, stubborn and argumentative. Or maybe I'm wrong and that is the way she always was. Or maybe her difficulties made her angry, and maybe feel incompetent, or made her feel unable to accomplish or do the things she wanted to.

In late December of 2004 Fran and I went to Bellevue Hospital to apply for a permit for disability parking. Her neurologist recommended this as Fran was having difficulty walking long distances and would tire easily. We had a letter from him and other documents to prove and support his recommendation. We made an appointment to see a doctor from the Department of Traffic and when we got there we were handed a questionnaire for Fran to fill out. It was designed to gauge the mental capacity of the person requesting the permit. One of the questions asked for the current date, which Fran did not know, and the name of New York City's mayor, which Fran did not remember. She asked me for the date and the name of the mayor. I told her I didn't know them and she argued with me and became very angry because at first she couldn't remember what she felt should be something she should know, and second that I wouldn't give her the answers. I tried to explain that not knowing the answers was how you pass this test but she couldn't comprehend that. She was livid and if we were not in a public setting things would have gotten very anxious. Luckily we were interrupted when the doctor became available to see her. She passed the exam by failing to answer the questions and the doctor who examined her approved her application for the permit. After we got home she wrote about the experience:

1) Going to the State Doctor's office made me feel like crying. Why? Because I felt like I was being treated like an idiot. Why? Because I'm not working & it made me aware that I'm nobody & that I have a progressing disease! This trip reminded me of the progression and I felt sick and sorry for myself. Also very stupid & forgetful. 2) I don't need to feel that way. I'm lucky. I have Moshe! & I can have a wonderful rest of life. 3) I feel fat & ugly! I keep gaining weight! I need more control of my life! Like Moe said. Go to the gym.

This was a very difficult period because it was impossible to understand what was happening to Fran. At first she seemed contrary and stubborn but I did not realize that it was more than that. She began to forget dates such as her birth date, and she couldn't remember names of people we had known for years, such as our neighbors and friends. She would pester me time and again to tell her the names of people we would see on the street. I couldn't understand her not knowing their names so I told her to forget calling them by name and just say "Hi." For some reason she couldn't do that and she couldn't explain her need to know their names. She would just ask again and again, "What are their names?" I didn't understand what her problem was and by the time we walked past our neighbors we were both angry.

These changes didn't occur overnight, but slowly and over several years. She took copious notes and then didn't know what they were for or she would try and use memory aids but had trouble concentrating so they were not of much use to her.

She began to make lists of the people on the block and their address, doctors and their phone numbers, people she was working with at the CUNY graduate school on her home ownership survey. Time and place began to lose meaning. Her vocabulary shrank. She began to hoard things, pencils, pens, paper for notes, folders and binders, almost anything. The whole thing must have been very frustrating for her, but I didn't realize that. I was too close to the subject and didn't see the whole picture because of all the small disturbing details. I also was very busy trying to keep our lives together, caring for Fran as we spent more time together. I didn't have the time to analyze our situation.

We still got away on summer weekends to our bungalow in the Catskills. It was while we were driving in our car that Fran's incontinence became an issue. She would tell me that she had to go to the bathroom and I would look for a likely place to stop. A gas station, diner, restaurant, anyplace with a bathroom. If we were lucky we found a place while she still had control of her bladder. There was a tension at these times, to get to a bathroom soon enough. Fran began to get quiet and I began to drive more quickly. These were difficult traveling experiences that went on for several years. To deal with Fran's incontinence I purchased an absorbent pad for her car seat and eventually bought several for use at home. I really didn't want Fran to wear diapers. Maybe because I am opposed to the throw away mentality in our society or it might be a way of denying the illness. Anyway, to deal with the problem in bed I devised an ingenious solution. A plastic sheet about two feet by three feet is placed on the bed where Fran would lay. On that plastic sheet I place a towel that is folded into three layers and then lay a towel over that. This has worked very well over the years as Fran does not move when she lies in bed. Most nights she will only soil those two towels. I have used this method, very effectively, for more than six years now. Ah, but when we got to the Catskills, things were easier and better, even though she couldn't remember our neighbors there and we continued that little battle it was a simpler and relaxed atmosphere.

Over the summer of 2006 I thought it would be a good idea to get away to someplace new and we drove to Prince Edward Island. We enjoyed our time together. Fran appreciated my caring for her and taking care of all the trip plans. She seemed very relaxed and I enjoyed the time with her and showering her with attention. As I remember it now, she seemed more passive than usual and less talkative during this trip.

It was also during this period that Fran began to have another physical problem that was very debilitating. Nausea. It would come upon her without warning and it made her very uncomfortable. When this occurred she would usually have to lie down to rest. We could never tell when the nausea would occur so we started to keep a daily record of medications, meals, symptoms, pains, emotional state, sleeping and awake activities. It was around this time that the PD really took control and determined the direction of our lives.

CHAPTER 23

Fran had nausea several times a day that caused extreme discomfort and it was painful to see her at these times. You never knew how long it would last or its severity. We tried over the counter antacids as well as a drug that was illegal in the USA that we ordered over the internet from Canada. Nothing worked but Ginger Ale soda seemed to help the most. We tried to track her daily activities to determine what might be causing it. Her neurologist and our regular doctor referred us to gastroenterologists. They probed her and pushed tubes down her throat and nose but no physical condition was discovered that would cause the nausea. We also discussed the problem with our dentist and periodontist. The opinion of all these medical professionals was that it was the PD that was causing the nausea. It was a neurological problem.

Dr. Lechtenberg had been seeing Fran for over six years at which time he wrote that she "…has a chronic neurologic condition which is progressive and incurable and results in physical impairment. She requires frequent medication, has problems with short term memory and fatigues quickly in terms of both her physical and mental functioning."

This must have been a very low point for Fran for it was at this time that she wrote this about us:

Anxiety, October, 2006
Feeling extremely anxious in regards to my husband's way of treating me. When I'm away from home doing things that make me feel satisfied, and special I don't feel frightened, palpitations banging against my chest.

I think I'm also depressed at times because I get very tired (although when the drugs kick in, I do feel better) if I'm not with him when he's talking about how I don't listen to him, (he lets me know that he tells me where items in the refrigerator belong and I don't put them in the right place). Other incidents of not listening to him include putting papers on the wall in the bungalow in the Catskills that have the names and other information about people in the bungalow colony; saying things are bad when they are not, such as he said, I know the lists of names shouldn't be on the wall.

We've been talking and things seem to be going well. I say something like let's go to a store, restaurant, ride in the car and somehow the words I used or the way I used them changed the awareness that things were going well. I get scared and interrupt him, which he sees as not listening and he begins to get louder and louder and my heart pounds more and my teeth begin grinding as I think about how cruel he is to me. When he is angry at my behavior he starts to talk about the past and how I didn't come down from my office when he picked me up at my office in the summer to go to the Catskills bungalow colony 10 years ago.

He is furious over this today and then he talks about how I lie when I spoke to Audrey Flores (who works with me on exercises). I told her that I was sorry I was late when she called to complain she was waiting for me to do exercises with her. I told her it was raining and crowded on the highway and I'd be there in a few minutes. Yes I gave an excuse that wasn't correct, but he uses it to show how I lie to people many times.

He stopped talking to me at lunch and dinner and he reads magazines and papers while I sit near him and eat. We talk less and less and in a way I am glad because when he gets very angry about something he feels I did, everything changes and I get sick, my heart pounds and his anger scares me particularly when he grabs my arms with fury and I feel he's going to hurt me. If this happens in the late evening I can't sleep, I have no energy, I can't concentrate on reading or much of anything. He also gets angry when I ask him people's names and lately he has stopped telling me. My memory seems to be increasingly limited which makes me feel lost. I don't feel that this memory loss which is growing is my fault. Yes, I'm not doing well but it's not because I don't listen. Moe thinks it is. I think I don't agree rather than I don't listen.

There are other illness related issues such as nausea, exhaustion, and feeling that I'm no good when Moe tells me repeatedly how limited my abilities are. I tend to slow down, my shoulders lean forward and I shuffle keeping my head down. As I write this I feel angry as hell wanting to feel strong and good about myself. Yes I have some problems that relate to the way I worked for 20 years that now make him furious—I worked continually, sometimes 7 days a week—but I can't understand why today we can't work to make us work. I do feel angry so much as I write this, that part of me doesn't want to have anything to do with him any more. The poor guy has had a life where the wife makes the money and the guy has had jobs but without huge pressures and with lots of time with his friends playing golf. As my mother used to say to me "my heart bleeds borscht for you."

I've had PD since I was 55 and I'm 64. I want to feel good about myself not the feeling I have of failure or feeling guilty or being unable to sleep or being unable to walk up the block without being out of breath. At another period in my life, other relationships including a bad marriage at age 19 to 22, life went on and I went

into therapy and made it through. Now I don't have the
skills I had. I'm sick much of the time and feeling sorry
for myself especially in the "off state." I feel I don't have
much time and to live with a man who sees my behavior
as an unwillingness to listen and yells at me most of the
time at times in which I feel sorry that I spoke at all.

I want to have a good life for the next 10 years. I want
to play scrabble with friends, sing, dance, play in my garden and have fabulous sex and delicious dinners in great
restaurants. I need support, I love all my exercise classes
but always feel like I wish I could feel good as I left and
went home to a pretty awful place to be. I start to feel
that I don't want to be with anyone and just be alone
especially since my husband is going out with friends
without me and sitting on the stoop so much of the time
without me. I want to go and be with people. I've started
talking about how sad and miserable I am, which is not
something I wanted to do with friends. Going to the
Brooklyn Mark Morris Dancers where they teach people
with PD dancing, singing and exercise makes me feel
better but Moe doesn't come with me any more because he doesn't want to be involved in any of this any
more. Sometimes I cry on the way to class because I
miss him now that he doesn't go with me to any classes
and how awful it is when I get home. I hope we can get
back together and enjoy the years we have left.

I thought you should hear from Fran. What she thought of
her diminished abilities, about my not helping her and our fighting, and her hopes for the future. You might think this is really
bad. But it was only the beginning of what became a consuming
struggle to maintain a semblance of normalcy while being bat-
tered by this illness. Everything one does or plans is dictated
by the illness. We put our faith in the doctors that the medicine
they prescribe will correct a problem and maybe make it go

away.The daily schedule was dictated by the medicines and the difficulties with PD when it would appear, and it was never shy.

CHAPTER 24

It was during 2007 that Fran began to have PD problems that lasted for long periods or kept reappearing throughout the day. She was constantly on edge about the next appearance of pain or nausea. It was sometime during the middle of 2007 that Fran changed neurologists. She had been talking with the members of the Parkinson's women's group about her nausea and they advised her to switch doctors as her current neurologist couldn't resolve her pain issue. They suggested she see a neurologist that most of the women in the group were seeing, Dr. — at the NYU Medical Center, and they were very pleased with the results of his treatment. We changed neurologists.

Fran's medications were constantly changing as the PD kept advancing slowly, imperceptibly. When diagnosed Fran was prescribed, at various times, Eldepryl, Symmetrel, Amantadine, Mirapex, and Selegeline. When we met Dr. — for the first time he recommended that Fran take Stalevo. After being on this drug for a week Fran's behavior changed and became bizarre. She now became curious about everything around her. Opening drawers and doors, checking what was in the cupboards and refrigerator. She was always moving, hyper, and I had to watch her because her activity worried me. I didn't understand what was happening and thought she might break things or hurt herself. The drug she was taking made her act as though she were on stimulants. In a restaurant having dinner with Sarah and myself she set fire to a napkin, laughing all the while, and saying how pretty it looked. I called Dr. — and told him I was stopping the Stalevo. He agreed and Fran returned to a mix of Sinamet, Mirapex and Zelapar. The Zelapar was very expensive and after two months of use, and not seeing any advantage to its use, I conferred with Dr. — and we went back to using Selegeline and Clonozapam. Fran was also told to take ibuprofen for the pain she frequently had in her neck and jaw, but that hardly ever worked for her.

It was also at this time that Fran exhibited some new and strange behaviors. She no longer had an assistant helping her with her personal business. She would sit at her desk for hours, shuffling papers, constantly organizing and reorganizing I don't know what. I tried talking to her and told her I would be glad to help her organize the information, one folder at a time. Eventually she relented. One of the folders we looked at contained information that was nine years old. There were notices for meetings, agendas, notes that Fran had taken, minutes of the meetings. I told Fran that this was really old stuff and she didn't need to save it anymore. I could see she was uncertain about what to do so I said to her, "Fran. This material is no longer important. The meeting happened nine years ago while you were working at NHS. You don't need this anymore. Now you are retired, not working at this job, so you can throw this stuff out." But she couldn't and I became angry and she became sullen and then several days later she asked, "Moe, can you help me with some of my work. I'm having trouble with it and I know you could help me."

"Fran," I said, "don't you remember I tried to help you several days ago and you couldn't take my advice. I looked over a lot of your papers and tried to tell you what you no longer needed and should get rid of but you didn't."

She said things would be different this time. I tried. Things weren't different and we fought. At least I got angry and frustrated and Fran just withdrew. Dr. —, after hearing our story, suggested to Fran that she use me like a secretary and that I could make her life easier that way and she should let me help her but she couldn't change. I didn't understand.

While trying to help Fran organize her "stuff" I noticed that she had several cups and trays filled with pencils, pens, and markers. I suggested that she give them to NHS or some other organization that could put them to good use. I told her the ball point pens would become useless because the ink in the pens would dry out before she would ever get to use them. I gathered them together with rubber bands for her. There were about 50 pencils, 60 pens, and 20 markers. I helped unclutter her desk and showed her how I had grouped the writing implements together. She said she would think about what to do with them and placed them in the back of her filing cabinet. I found them there two years later while trying to clean up her work area. I didn't understand.

And then, one evening while putting away some of her laundry in her sock drawer, I noticed a small coin purse. Thinking Fran had placed it in the wrong drawer and wouldn't find it if she were to look for it I picked it up and looked to see what was in it. There were a variety of multi colored pills. I recognized some as prescription drugs and the others could have been anything, supplements or ibuprofen. I panicked as she could take these incorrectly or at the wrong time. I didn't understand why Fran would have secreted these pills. I then checked several other of her clothing drawers and found additional caches of pills in the toes of some of her socks, in small pill containers hidden amongst her underwear, wrapped in tissue paper and placed in the corner of the drawers. She saw me as I was finding them and asked what I was doing. I told her that I was taking these pills because if she ever needed pills she would find any that she needed in the cupboard in the kitchen. "You don't have to hide them around the house. The doctors told us what pills to use and when to take them. There is no need to keep private groups of pills in separate places." She either didn't understand what I was saying or didn't care. I couldn't rationally explain it in a way she could agree to. I wanted to take the pills that I found and throw them out. I didn't know what they were for or how old they were. I couldn't let Fran take these suspect pills so I decided to throw them out. Fran became very upset and physically tried to take the pills back. We fought. I took the pills away. That night I moved all the pills in the cupboard to a new spot that was too high for Fran to reach. Several days later she asked me where the pills were and why I hid them from her. I told her that I would provide her with everything she needed everyday but that didn't satisfy her and we fought again. Just screaming this time and not physical. Later that night, while Fran was sleeping, I moved all the pills to the basement where Fran never went so I wouldn't have to worry about her taking pills she didn't need. I didn't understand.

Another evening while I was putting away the laundry, I do a wash every day now, and hanging up Fran's nightgown I noticed a lump in the pocket of her bathrobe. It was a roll of bills totaling $1,800. What a surprise. That wasn't what I said though when I took the roll and divided it placing $800 back in the robe. Throughout our married life I would always manage our finances. I made certain that there was cash in the house, which I kept it in my sock drawer, and if either Fran or Sarah needed cash they would take what they needed. When it ran low I would go to the bank and refill our supply. I never noticed that the money was being depleted quickly so Fran must have been taking money over a long period and hiding it. The next day she came to me and said she was missing money but didn't accuse me. She even showed me that it was in her robe. I couldn't admit to taking it so I told her she must be mistaken and it must be in some other garment. And surprisingly there was more money that she had hidden with her clothing. She didn't want me to search her dresser drawers but I wouldn't be denied. Here too she had hidden money in various denominations from singles to several hundred dollar bills. In all I found that she had squirreled away over $5,000. I don't know how long it must have taken her to accumulate so much cash but she was very upset that I was finding "her" money. As I kept uncovering more cash I became certain that she no longer knew where she had hidden much of it. I told her that it didn't make much sense to keep it in the house and that we should put it in a savings account in a bank where she would earn interest. I don't understand why she agreed to do this but we went to the bank the next day and made a deposit into our account and she never brought the subject of money up again except for saying, at times, that she didn't have any money. I didn't understand.

At the end of 2007 and into 2008 I noticed that Fran was beginning to walk much slower and carefully. She had balance problems that her medication seemed to help somewhat but never enough. There was always a drug wearing off period and her symptoms would return. We began tracking her days and started keeping a log. She was now aware that her memory was failing and I was unaware how much this troubled her. I couldn't get a handle onto what was happening. In the past Fran and I had differences of opinions on issues and now when I didn't understand some of the things Fran was doing I still thought that it was just a matter of a difference of opinion. I was wrong. There was something going on that I didn't understand. Friends and neighbors also noticed a change in Fran that they thought was depression and suggested that she see a psychiatrist. I thought it couldn't hurt so I found a recommended psychotherapist in the neighborhood. We visited her twice, together, to introduce Fran and try and define her situation. After that Fran would go on her own. Several months later the therapist asked to see me. She wanted to discuss why Fran was always bringing up how difficult I was and what I could do to make her situation better. I got a bit defensive and told her that I thought Fran was controlling the session by pointing it away from herself and that she should try and get her back to a more productive topic. Several months later the therapist called while Fran was in a session to tell me she had collapsed and I should come and help her home. This occurred several more times either because of a drug situation or stress at the therapists office. I decided that Fran should no longer see the therapist.

The nausea discomfort was diminishing and eventually disappeared. It was sometime during 2008 that PD traded problems. It started out slowly, as all PD problems do, and continued to escalate, pain in the neck, throat, gums, and mouth. We tried acupuncture for the pain. It didn't work. I made appointments for Fran at the Albert Ellis Institute for Biofeedback sessions. We stopped after four sessions at the suggestion of the counselor we were seeing because Fran was not able to concentrate on the directions she was given. Fran only wanted to discuss, it seemed, how we weren't getting along. I started keeping a daily log again, and tracked the data for two months. I would present it to our neurologist at our next appointment. This is what it looked like.

9/20/09   8:40   1/2 a Sinamet, can't walk, no balance, can't sit up. This seems to be happening more frequently.

9:00   Balance returns and can talk but by 9:30 begins to feel sick.

10:30   After b'kfast nausea sets in. Shortly after very sick, can't move, can't lift head and can't sit upright. 1/2 Sinamet. To bed.

1:15   Ate out—appetite okay.

1:50   Begins to feel neck pain—pressure, collapses. 1/2 Sinamet. Walk home 6 blocks with difficulty. Shows PD gait. In bed by 2:30.

5:30   Wakes up dazed, difficult moving, sleeps on back with mouth open.

9:10   Start of down period 1/2 Sinamet. Sparks up after 20 minutes and holds animated conversation. Walks okay.

11:00   1/2 Sinamet then goes to bed.

12:30   Goes to bathroom on her own—feels okay.

9/21/09   8:30   1/2 Sinamet—20 minutes pass and then can dress self, walk, animated, good appetite.

9:30   Starts to feel ill but does not collapse. Has difficulty breathing and says face feels like it is filling up.

11:00   Goes to bed—1/2 Sinamet.

1:30   Awakes. 1/2 Sinamet. Lunch. Good appetite. Go

for walk, get ice cream

3:30   Feels terrible, back in bed.

6:00   1/2 Sinamet. Still feels bad and goes back to sleep.

7:20   Woke her up for dinner. Still feels bad.

8:00   Had wine with meal. Blames wine for mouth hurts, can't talk.

8:45   Sits stationary with blank stare. Asks to go to hospital. Blank face, no voice, needs to drink through straw 1/2 Sinamet.

9:10   Starts to look up and eyes move.

11:00 Awoke and walked to bathroom without assistance. All affect looks good—smiles.

9/23/09   7:00   Can't move or roll over in bed.

7:30   1/2 Sinamet—shower needs total assistance.

8:10   Self sufficient.

9:00   Go to P/T appointment. Looks okay.

9:30   Begins to feel sick. 1/2 Sinamet.

11:15 Sinamet did not take effect till now. Fran cleans in yard.

12:00 Eats lunch with gusto.

1:00   Begins to fade 3-1/2 hours after 9:30 dose. 1/2 Sinamet. Pain in mouth. Takes nap.

3:30   Still not feeling well. Can't talk or move. Has no affect. 1/2 Sinamet.

Once again we saw numerous doctors, dentists, oncologists, and nothing physically was detected that would cause her complaints. The pain would occur several times each day. Fran was now having more difficulty remembering names or places or how to use the appliances at home. The PD had seeped into every crevice of our lives. Our days were devoted to managing Fran's condition and it consumed all of our thoughts, energy, and time. We were always looking for an answer to why these things would happen to her. We were advised to take a gluten allergy test and one for Lyme disease. Both were negative. After a while you begin to realize that things will not get better. That is what a degenerative disease is all about and this day is still the best you can expect. It took me a long time to reach this point. Much too long. But the disease is not really noticeable as there are no broken bones and plaster casts to see. There are no blood soaked bandages to change. No fever to test for. There are only indeterminate physical symptoms that the doctors try to alleviate with drugs. That is what doctors do. But the drugs are very powerful and don't always work as hoped for. Since the disease is always progressing the choice and dose of the drugs is always changing as well. And I never was told or remembered or was made to understand that Parkinson's can also cause dementia.

CHAPTER 25

Caring for Fran all these years has been challenging. Trying to keep up with her changes, and not doing a great job at times, was frustrating and tiring. Friends and neighbors would ask how things were going and "How is Fran doing?" How many times do you say "Okay." before you begin to say the truth, "Not so good."

I will encapsulate our life as briefly as I can with thoughts on Fran's condition around November of 2009. No two days are ever exactly the same. We awake in the morning between seven and eight and Fran has not had any medication for about 10 hours. She is very docile, moves slowly, seems confused and her balance is somewhat impaired. She talks softly, if at all. Takes her first dose of sinamet at 7:30–8 am. I help her getting dressed with most of her clothing. She can do things for herself. I let her but it takes longer and she may not succeed and will then need assistance. 15 to 20 minutes after she has taken her medicine she freezes and stares off into space or will hum. You can sense the drug is hitting her brain cells with force. She will sit this way for about 10 minutes and then Fran becomes mobile and active. We are usually sitting at the kitchen table and she does most things for herself here although there is always some confusion. Even with food in front of her she will try and get food from other peoples plates. More than one plate or glass in front of her confuses her and she seems not to know what to grab for. After about an hour and a half she begins to complain about pains and tiredness. She may have difficulty moving or move slowly. Usually she will fall asleep in the chair she is sitting on or go to bed. I will try to give her medication every 2 and a quarter to 2 and a half hours. The timing does not seem to have any effect. Sometimes after taking her medication she will not recover and will still feel poorly.

Physically Fran may awake with a foot cramp. Most of the

time it will go away after I massage it for 10 minutes. Drugs don't seem to make any difference. She does pee in bed about once every five days. This is not a problem with our towel technique for absorbing the urine. Fran's medicine's seems to work okay when things are going okay. But Fran is never really okay for any length of time. She may be okay for an hour or so and then not feel well for anywhere from 1/2 an hour to three hours. At this time she will sleep. Sometimes she feels well enough to go for five or six hours, never feeling great yet never so bad she collapses. She has pains in her throat, jaw, neck, mouth, head, that we treat with ibuprofen or acetaminophen. This helps sometimes but she always says that they make her pain worse, not realizing that the medicine takes time to have an effect, if at all. At these times we have fights due to her confusion about taking the pill and not wanting to take the pill, and my insisting she give it back to me if she does not take it and her refusal to do so.

Almost daily she may get tired and need to nap. Her hands might cramp. To sum up, there seems to be no predictable result from her taking medication or to be prepared for what each day may bring. The pains she has from her neck up seem to cause her the most distress. She still has nausea at times. She has vision problems that I don't know what to attribute to. She is also constipated and tries to manage this by herself so I am not aware of the extent of the problem at all times. She will drool sometimes when she is in extreme distress and her medicines are in an off stage. Her speech is also very low at times. She has no problem sleeping.

Generally Fran is not a depressed person but at times she becomes depressed. Here, also, no two days are the same but there are similarities. Fran worries about everything, has anxiety attacks, and is very forgetful. She can't remember the names of friends or neighbors. She was aware of her abilities failing her when she wrote Dr. — this note on January 3, 2009.

I feel worse and worse. I have lots of "down" periods

during the day and I hate it. I have good periods too. I can't remember people's names. My vocabulary in general is harder to access. I have bad pain in my neck muscles. I can't remember how to do the simple neck stretches, nor can I remember to do them at all. The pain in my neck affects my whole head. I feel like I can't breath. It is scary. Chewing gum seems to help lately. I am obsessed with organizing all the papers I have from my career, but I can't do it alone. I want it organized so I can find things, but it will take a lot of work to do. I work and work on it and it is very stressful. I feel like I have so much work to do and I am overwhelmed and stressed out all the time about it. I spend a lot of time looking for things that I lose and panicking about it. It is awful.

Fran now forgets the names of foods. When in a restaurant she tries to read the entire menu and I think this is because she is confused and doesn't understand what she is reading. We can't order until she goes over the entire menu. I don't know if she understands or can read the menu for she doesn't communicate what she is reading. She continually looks at the menus pages, maybe reading, without being able to make a decision. I may make a suggestion and she will ask me to repeat it and describe what the item is and eventually she will accede to my choice.

She has heart palpitations and many times tells me that she cannot breath, but of course she does. This sometimes occurs when she has the neck pains and at these times she may ask, repetitively, and annoyingly to take her to a doctor or hospital.

She has been in a hospital twice and was tested for heart attack. The tests showed she didn't have a heart problem but she continued to complain, at times, that she couldn't breath and wanted to go to the hospital. When that occurred I would try to calm her and work with her to breath deeply and relax. At times she would physically try and leave where we were, in our home, our car, a restaurant, and I would restrain her and try and get her to relax. These were stressful times for both of us.

She will ask me to explain the same thing numerous times, (such as the difference between the over the counter drugs she takes, phone numbers of friends, schedule of when she takes drugs, names of people in groups she attends) over a period of weeks, months, and wants me to write it down for her. I have told her that she would be better off not trying to do this and just trust me to help her when she needs help. It takes too much time to repetitively do these tasks and I refuse to repeat them.

Fran sometimes has trouble knowing where she is. She asks if we are home or when are we going home when we are at our home. She sometimes asks if we are married and doesn't seem to believe it when I tell her we are and for how long.

Her ability to be interested in something depends on whether she likes it. She can garden and sit at her desk and review papers that should have been trashed years ago. She constantly is reorganizing her papers and lists without apparent purpose. This activity seems to have lessened over the past several months. She is obsessive and stubborn. She will pick up every leaf on our sidewalk and refuse to stop either until she is done or she collapses with fatigue. She constantly reorganizes her three drawer dresser that contains socks, underwear, pocketbooks, wallets, and some pictures. She has begun, at times, to eat using her fingers more than utensils.

She either disregards what I ask or doesn't hear what I say. In either case this will, often lead to confrontations that can become physical.

She has problems with processes, such as turning on the stove and setting the height of the flame, using a computer, sorting mail, cutting vegetables.

Managing Fran's needs on a daily basis is a difficult and draining occupation. I have thought that we might move into an assisted living arrangement. I checked the costs of that and a nursing home. I asked her neurologist for some suggestions based on his experience and knowledge. What should I expect in the future? What costs will I incur? Who to contact about setting up a home environment? Any resources to be directed to? He did direct me to a social worker on staff who managed these issues. I was referred to publications by the National Parkinson's Foundation that covered all aspects of the illness that one might encounter. I read books about medicines and treatments written by doctors, guides for the patient and family, questions and answers. One of the best books was "Defending Against The Enemy" by Eric Morgan. But talking and reading about PD and living with it are two very different scenarios.

CHAPTER 26

Starting in 2010 things were to become even more difficult and challenging. Thinking of the glass as either half full or half empty I can define this period as either difficult years with some good days in between or just your average good years with some terrible days occurring. This was the time when Fran was really changing and I couldn't comprehend what was happening to her. Her skills, personality, charm, and abilities were shrinking and her needs growing.

I can't begin to enumerate all of the difficulties and changes that Fran experienced over time due to her illness. Her symptoms were very different from the people in our support group who mostly had movement difficulties. Fran also exhibited a loss of the interactive and interpersonal skills she once possessed. I took her to three other neurologists for their diagnoses and opinions. They all concluded she had atypical Parkinsonism with prominent non-motor symptoms. She showed atypical cognitive deficits particularly "frontal" (whatever that means) along with her being "nearly mute but capable of speech." I now realized there was nothing anyone could do that would make things better for Fran and by extension, myself.

Doctors are strange people. But not unlike other professions where one aspires to succeed for all that it will provide. Hopefully, financial comfort, peer approval, prestige, respect for the title, unquestionable knowledge and authority. I know that is a generalization but this is my story and I can do that. When we first met Dr. — he spent a lot of time interviewing Fran, getting her history, taking many notes, so I thought, "This seems promising." After seeing him for several years I began to think he was losing interest in us as patients. Could it be that Fran was not responding to the treatment in a way he wanted? At each appointment an assistant would ask us questions from a prepared questionnaire and for Fran to do some physical tasks. This took maybe half an hour or so and then we would see him and he would look over the answers that we gave his assistant and continue the appointment. I began to feel that we were part of a study he was conducting and maybe we weren't providing the proper results. Oh, I almost forgot. He wasn't the promptest of physician's. We were always on time for the appointments that he had set, yet he always kept us waiting. I asked him about this. Very politely I said, "You know we have been waiting for over an hour to see you and this isn't the first time this has happened. It is hard for Fran to sit immobile while her drugs are doing their thing. It also isn't considerate of the time I spend to bring Fran in for her appointment and take her home." The doctor explained that sometimes there are emergencies that are unaccounted for that he has to attend to. There have been other times when other doctors have used the exact same words to me. There must be a class 'Excuses 101' or something like that. The next appointment was no different and I said the same thing to the doctor about making us wait. I tried to adjust Fran's medication so she would be up for the appointment but could not count on the doctor to be on time. I was very annoyed and again complained and the response was something like, "Sometimes things come up that I have no control over." I then said, "This time we waited for over one hour to see you. You set the time of the appointment. You have a college and medical school education as your wall can attest to. Yet you can't maintain your schedule for your patients. Patients who are waiting, many times uncomfortably because of their Parkinson's Disease, for your attention and expertise? That is unacceptable to people who are very sick and come to you for help. It is rude to think that your time is more valuable than theirs. I just want you to know this is not the way to treat your patients." He told me in no uncertain terms that if I didn't like it I should find another doctor. So that is what I did and I am much happier now because my wait time is more reasonable.

It was during this period that Fran became argumentative and physical. In our study we each had a desk to work on and

Fran had been working at hers since she retired, in 2003. At first she really was working at her desk because she was part of the team at CUNY completing the survey on home ownership. After 2007 she would still work there organizing her papers and folders. By 2009 all she would do is shuffle the same papers that were on her desk, day after day, and never even open her file cabinet.

Talking to Fran and trying to reason with her was useless. At times she did not talk; she was non-communicative. There were times she would enter our study and sit down at my desk. "Francine," I would say. "You are sitting at my desk and your desk and papers are right there," pointing to her desk. She acted as though she didn't hear me and would begin to mess with the papers, rolodex, calendar, folders, etc., on my desk. "Francine, those are papers that I am working on please don't mess them up. Please stop what you are doing and go to your desk." But she never understood what I was saying or just refused to do what I asked for and I physically would have to move her so that she wouldn't disrupt my work space. She would fight back sometimes and I would forcibly take her out of the study. Eventually, to prevent fights, I placed a lock on the door to the study. We then had arguments, verbal and physical, about my locking the room, keeping her out, and she wanting to get in.

Fran has some minor skin discoloration spots on her face. She began to spread soap, toothpaste, or any other salve or ointment that she found in the medicine cabinet on her face. At first I tried to explain to her what the products were for and not everything should be smeared on her face. I finally realized she wouldn't or couldn't understand the explanation so I took all of the paraphernalia in the medicine cabinet and hid it in a box at the top of a closet.

At times Fran would get out of bed in the middle of the night and start looking into her dresser and night table. She would pull out her clothes and try and reorganize her socks and underwear. Nothing could stop her from these activities once she started. Only when she became tired or exhausted would I be able to get her back into bed. She would also go downstairs to the kitchen, look in the refrigerator, I don't know what for. I would stop her before she started removing food. We would fight and I would stand between her and the fridge until I finally got her to go back to bed.

There were times that she thought the kitchen garbage can was her bathroom toilet and would start to pull her pants down as she rushed towards it. The first time she did this surprised me but I learned quickly to steer her towards the bathroom when this occurred again. She thought she was doing the appropriate thing and we struggled when I tried to change her direction to go to the bathroom. She did not want to sit on the toilet seat and would keep trying to stand up. And so we fought.

She forgot what the purpose of things were or how to use them. Five out of six times she forgets how to use toilet paper. When told to drop the toilet paper into the toilet she looks around for the proper place which to her could be a small trash can or the toilet brush holder or she just looks around confused not doing anything. She repeatedly tore the toilet paper holder off the wall. I didn't replace it after this happened three times. She tore a towel rack off the wall. She has forgotten, at times, how to turn on the faucet, and tries twisting the handle in ways that I think will break it. She has tried to open the medicine cabinet by pulling the door off of its hinges. She tries to remove the design on our dinnerware by scraping it with her utensils. She has broken our window blinds and tried to tear down the curtains. And so we fight. I think I've said enough about these topics.

I didn't want to change the space we have been living in for the past 40 years. It is our home. I am very comfortable here and so is Fran. The question was how to live with Fran without making too many changes. So I hid a couple of the things that she focused and obsessed over or that could have caused her harm or me anxiety. I placed things out of her sight or reach. I removed objects from the environment, such as furniture that she might trip over or that she might inadvertently knock over and break. Always trying to be vigilant to the disruptions that could ruin the day.

We had many fights over the years, as often as once a week, and they seemed to arise spontaneously. They could be violent. I would try to constrain her and prevent her from doing something that would either make my life more miserable or difficult or could put her in danger. But she was unstoppable and determined when she decided to do something and there was no reasoning with her. She would keep pushing to get her way and I was, many times, in her way. I have scars where she bit and scratched me. She pulled hair from my head and tore my clothing. She would kick me and grab my fingers and try to bend them backwards. It ended by my either shoving her down or punching or slapping her to get her to stop what she was doing. That usually didn't change her behavior. She would sometimes become more furious and I would try and restrain her. I wanted to immobilize her for both our sakes. She was becoming more argumentative, stubborn, and difficult. Not at all the woman I knew and I was becoming more frustrated and didn't understand the changes that were occurring in her and my inability to deal with them. So I began to hold her firmly when we would have a disagreement and she couldn't strike me or continue doing what I deemed as "not too good." Eventually she would tire, this did not always happen quickly. But within half an hour after the incident, she forgot it. But I didn't.

I eventually learned to have patience with her or to distract her from what she was doing that was problematic. In most instances, but not all of the time, this worked for me and Fran.

CHAPTER 27

It took me several years to come to terms with Fran's condition. I finally understood that I had to change my behavior because she couldn't change hers. I needed to be patient with Fran and the things she did because, it finally penetrated, I understood, she now had minimal control over her physical and mental actions.

It is now 2010 and I realize I will have to change things to make our lives as easy as I can make it. Amongst the many people I met who were the caregivers to their spouse there were only three, I felt, that understood what we were going through and could share and verbalize it in a way that was critical yet sympathetic. We would meet in support groups or coffee shops and talk about what was happening in our lives. There must have been something, maybe similar, in our personalities that helped us understand each other so that we could share and open up in ways that I did not find with others in the support groups. We talked about our emotional commitment, psychic pain, tiredness and stress, financial considerations, and physical environment changes that would be necessary.

I knew that Fran's physical space would have to change as her condition worsened. The duplex we lived in had the bathroom on the second floor where our bedroom is. I knew that sometime in the future Fran would not be climbing those stairs so during the summer of 2010 I hired a contractor who changed that bathroom into an accessible one without a bath tub and built a new bathroom on the first floor. I think that sometime down the road Fran and I will be living totally on the first floor so we will have our bedroom there as well. During the summer of 2010, while the work on our house was undertaken, we spent the summer in our getaway bungalow. We also spent the summers of 2011 and 2012 in our bungalow as life seems easier there. We have a swimming pool for the hot days and the nights always cooled off and sleeping was very comfortable, without the need for an air conditioner. The space is fairly small, about 350 square feet, and there is a screened in porch. Everything we need is close by. Shopping is about four miles away and convenient. The public library has a large selection of books and DVDs with helpful librarians. It is an ideal place for us. I found that I could get along without a phone, we have no land line there and the cell service is spotty. Whenever I drive into town I check my cell phone for messages. We don't have a TV but we do have radio reception. I don't receive mail there (my daughter brings all of it to me when she comes to visit several times during the summer) but I do have internet access and pay my bills that way.

Fran was still mobile at this time. We would go shopping together and eat out at the neighborhood restaurants and diners. But Fran began to exhibit some difficult behaviors. While shopping she would fight with me about buying candy and cookies. In a restaurant, after finishing our meal, that always included a desert, if we had to pass the desert counter with its trays of cakes and donuts on the way out, Fran would not want to leave the restaurant until we bought something else. I then changed our eating habits and only ate in restaurants or pizza parlors that did not have a display counter with deserts. It was also at this time that I began to hire people to stay with Fran while I went shopping or did other chores. This was also the summer that we had sex for the last time. At the end of the summer when we returned to Brooklyn I began to hire people to stay with Fran for six hours a day, three days a week. This gave me the freedom to shop, go to the gym or golfing, or anything else I might want to do without concern about Fran's well being.

When we returned to Brooklyn many of our patterns were changing as well because they had to be tuned to Fran's abilities and when her medicine kicked in which determined her on/off periods. We stopped going to the Mark Morris dance classes because Fran would "crash" sometime during the class and I would have to just about carry her out of the studio. I could never adjust her medicine to a level that would properly manage the entire afternoon and so we would have to leave before the class ended. We continued to attend the singing classes as we would be seated there. Fran, however, could no longer sing along with the group. I am uncertain as to why this occurred but I think Fran was having difficulty using the song book. I would get her book to the page where the song we were singing was on but she just kept flipping through the pages and did not sing at all. At times, however, she would applaud the efforts of the piano player and he would note that "Fran liked that one."

Two of Fran's dear friends from her working days, Barbara Kent and Rick Roberto, stayed in touch and would visit us monthly and we would go out to a restaurant for an early dinner. Fran seemed to recognize them, but I'm not sure of that as she is very friendly to people that she meets and even greets strangers warmly and with a smile. She also loves and interacts with children between the ages of three to about seven. If we are in a restaurant she will smile at them and try to get their attention and wave. This seems odd, but that is where she is at.

At home, on a daily basis, our schedule is pretty much the same. We get up around 8 AM and she will take a Sinamet, her medicine. Her neurologist suggested she take the medication at four hour intervals and that is the only medicine she takes now. We then have breakfast and Fran is okay for about 2 hours and then she goes to sleep or naps. I will wake her at about noon for another dose of medicine and we have lunch. She is good till about 2:30 or 3 when she goes to sleep again. I will wake her at about 4 PM for her next dose and we will have dinner at about 5:30. She is good till about 6:45 and then she is off to bed and will generally sleep through the night. Sometimes she will deviate from the schedule and not sleep or nap during the day or just nap for a short period and then get up. She has to be watched most of the time when she is awake because you never know what she will do or try to take apart or lose her balance and fall. She can be distracted easily, most of the time, when she starts doing something destructive. The times that she can't be distracted are the times we have our confrontations. Luckily she does sleep a lot otherwise I would be totally exhausted by the end of day. After Fran is put to bed, at about 7 PM, I really don't want to do anything except chill and watch TV even though I know it is a wasteland. So it is then that I may try to do small unimportant chores that don't require too much thinking or effort, like paying bills. I'm satisfied with that.

At first I was annoyed that I was taking care of Fran and we had these moments, every couple of days, where she wouldn't listen to what I was asking of her. She would refuse to do, what I thought, were reasonable, rational, and simple requests that didn't require too much effort on her part. I didn't realize she couldn't process what I was asking of her and so we would fight. But she wasn't the only one who couldn't process what was going on. It took me a long time, too long really, for me to realize how much Fran had lost.

This brings us to another aspect of PD that is rarely discussed as one of the symptoms. DEMENTIA. It isn't a typo that I capitalized the word. I did that because it is a big deal. Like PD it is silent and progresses slowly. It is really difficult to try and understand what is happening. Dementia generally occurs after the a person has had PD for about 10 to 15 years. It is difficult to describe as it exhibits different symptoms in different people depending on which parts of the brain becomes impaired. Imagine that the brain is made up of 1,000 compartments or cells. Each with its own responsibility and function. Imagine that in order to accomplish these functions or jobs they are all interconnected both chemically and electronically via tubes and wires. It has to be whole and that means that all the connections and cells have to be functioning without missing a beat for us to consider everything is "normal". Imagine there is a short circuit in the wiring (the electronic part) of the brain or one of the tubes is clogged and blocked (the chemical part) or that a cell (the function part) is broken or dying. Then

all of those compartments that have specific duties and responsibilities are not communicating with each other as they need
to and so can't perform as well as they used to or can't perform
their function at all. Some of those compartments or cells deal
with memory and cognitive functions while others deal with
muscle control or physical functions such as balance or bladder
control or swallowing or blinking. Once these connections are
broken they can't be repaired by the medical knowledge we
currently possess and PD is a progressive degenerative disease.
It only gets worse.

CHAPTER 28

Since 2011 the days have all been rather similar. We wake at about the same time every day, take medication, eat meals, take rest periods, watch TV, and don't talk much. That's for Fran. My days, mostly, revolve around her needs and schedule. Of course I take care of myself as that is important, so my friends and neighbors keep reminding me. Some of the things I do, besides take care of Fran, is go to a gym about three times a week. I think this helps me stay strong and healthy so I can manage my days of taking care of Fran more easily. Play golf when the weather allows. I do the shopping and cooking and cleaning, because I have always done these things. The hardest thing to do is to realize that one shouldn't plan on keeping to firm schedules because that won't happen. It took me a long time to relax my expectations about managing the time when we would do things. Now, if we don't eat when expected or awake or go to bed at a set time, it doesn't matter. Relaxing with this uncertainty is a wonderful growth experience for me and I have almost mastered it. Even after Fran has taken her drugs I can't predict what will happen because the response is not always as expected. Sometimes, after 15 minutes or so her body may tense up and she will appear catatonic. At other times she may tense up but begin to hum or chant something unrecognizable. And sometimes after she takes her medicine she may become very active. And usually, shortly after taking her medicine, her appetite is voracious and she will devour her food, eating with utensils and her hands. It is all unpredictable.

That isn't totally true. I can predict that it will be difficult to have Fran do what I ask of her. I haven't yet decided whether she doesn't hear me, won't do what I ask of her, or doesn't understand what I am asking. But it really doesn't matter because her response rouses the ire in me. Well, that used to be what happened but I have changed in many ways. What I tell you now isn't all bad. Maybe sad.

I used to get upset when Fran would eat her meals with her hands. Now she will eat, at times, using her utensils and at other times using her hands but most of the time it will be a combination of both of those. The doctor says I should be grateful that she can feed herself. But she does make a mess. I tell myself not to worry about it and I will clean up after she finishes eating. I now know that she can't really help herself when she eats. I have thought of giving her only finger food so there wouldn't be such a mess but I haven't made that choice, yet. I still try and give her balanced and healthy meals that have nourishment and flavor.

She loves to look at photo albums but she began to tear the plastic sleeves and the photos. At first I tried to talk to her and asked her not to destroy the albums. I explained that the plastic was to protect the photos and the photos were valued remembrances. It took a while for me to realize she didn't know what she was doing and couldn't stop doing it. The solution was to hide the photo albums and replace them with magazines. Tearing apart magazines or newspapers is now one of her favorite activities. She concentrates on the tearing and becomes very involved with this work. It is one of her favorite activities and she can manage this for almost two hours before she has her PD collapse. This obsessive compulsive behavior takes place while working in the garden and pulling out weeds and plants that are not green and in the fall she will pick up leaves that have fallen from trees. She gets down on her hands and knees and will pick up every leaf she can reach until exhausted. I can't get her to use a broom. Maybe she has forgotten how to use one. I will try and help her by bringing her a bucket so she can place the leaves she collects into it and not have to hold them all in her hands. She seems to adjust to this solution easily and that's okay. She seems happy.

It might be a need to take things apart that is basic to her personality because she fiddles with the zippers on her clothes, the laces or ties on her shoes, the edge of blankets and cushions, the hems of pillow cases, and I could go on and on. When I see her doing something that might damage her clothing or our furniture I try to take it from her and if that doesn't work I try and distract her with something else. If that doesn't work I think of the new things I will eventually buy.

When she can dress herself it goes very slowly as though she is trying to figure out the way to do it and what goes where. Sometimes she is too stiff and doesn't have the movement range to put on her clothes. If allowed to pick out her own clothes she might put on three pair of underwear or both socks on one foot. There is confusion and all you can do is try and help patiently. Sometimes she won't allow you to help her and then you have to sit back for a minute or two. Usually she will let you help after a couple of minutes have passed. That might be because she forgets what or why she is doing something or it loses its importance to her.

I used to worry when she wet her pants. I would struggle with her to take her clothes off and many times she didn't want that. We would fight because I thought it would harm her to wear urine soaked clothing. We don't fight any more about that issue. I wait a minute or two and try again to change her clothing. That usually works but if it doesn't then it is better not to fight and she can walk around in wet clothes, for a while.

Sometimes, however, I can't give in to her. At times she can be unbelievably stubborn and then things get terribly difficult for both of us. One example, that doesn't occur frequently at all, thankfully, is when she defecates in her clothing. She will usually feel the urge and normally reaches the bathroom on time, but there are times when she doesn't quite make it. When this happens she wouldn't allow me to remove her soiled clothes. You can't fault me for trying. While attempting to remove her pants and undergarment she grabbed some toilet paper and wiped herself. I asked her, several times, to throw the soiled toilet paper into the toilet bowl and she didn't. Then the battle began. I couldn't get her to drop the soiled paper in the toilet bowl and couldn't get her to let me remove her pants.

This was a tough situation to be in and we struggled. She came up off the toilet seat and soiled that and the floor and her legs. I must have asked her 20 times, while holding her hands, to drop the paper and open her hand and she refused. I was careful not to let her bite me or grab my thumbs. After perhaps three minutes, it seemed longer, she became exhausted and gave up. I cleaned the toilet seat and floor. Washed her legs and hands and pants and underwear. I was angry and let her lie there on the bathroom floor for a good 10 minutes until I was calmer and then as she was exhausted and falling asleep I took her to bed.

There are times when she asks, "When are we going home?" while we are at home. There are times when she asks, When are we going to the meeting?" or "When are the people coming here?" At those times I simply tell her that we are home and that we don't have any meetings "today." That seems to satisfy her every time, it seems to calm her, and she doesn't pursue the issue. When we visit our neurologist she may point at me and asks Fran "Who is this man?" Fran looks bemused, usually, and if she does answer will say "That is my husband." Then the doctor will ask her "And what is his name?" and Fran can't find the answer. So I am the man she lives with, whom she says she loves, but can't recall my name.

I now know that many of the problems that Fran has are caused by either the PD or by the medications themselves. I am certain that it is these powerful drugs that affect her brain in ways that make her difficult, stubborn, and argumentative. Or maybe I'm wrong and that is the way she always was. Or maybe her difficulties are what makes her angry. All in all Fran is really having a very difficult time and I am unaware of what is going on in her body because she doesn't communicate verbally at all. She doesn't talk anymore in an understandable way and her thoughts when she does talk seem without context or a relationship to what is going on. Now you understand that the illness affects all activities that the brain can initiate or try and process. It can also alter the senses of smell, sight and taste. It is more complicated than you can imagine and no one can be prepared for it. It is like on the job training.

It is okay that not everything goes as smoothly as I would like. It really is. I work at keeping Fran in my thoughts as she used to be and remember why I loved and admired her. Pictures of us around the house, albums, and VCR tapes of our vacations help with this and even though she is a shell of who she was, our connection is still very strong. I know that our relationship seems one sided now for Fran has little to contribute and is very needy. I think a reasonable comparison would be of some guy who owns a car that he loves and cares for thoroughly and is out every weekend taking care of it. He washes and waxes the car. Checks the fluids and belts. Checks the air pressure in the tires and retouches little dings in the paint. Washes the white walls till they sparkle and cleans the interior. He puts all this energy and care into an inanimate object because it is what some guys do.

Well I take care of Fran the same way except she is not inanimate. That is aggravating at times but those times pass and the love I feel for her shines through. I know that she loves me, even though she exhibits bursts of anger at me through her frustrations, because she tells me so, many times each day. I know this is one of those times where she understands what she is saying. I can see it in her eyes. She also will easily fold within my arms whenever I embrace her. She will caress me and hold my hand whenever we are beside one another.

Fran and I have been very fortunate. We fell in love with each other on the day we met and never lost that feeling. We learned several techniques for getting over rough periods that further cemented our commitment and the desire to make the relationship work. We did many things together and many separately. We each followed different paths in our professional lives. Most importantly, even though we had different interests we shared common values and respected and trusted each other. I remember one trip we took in Europe. As I was looking at the art work in the museums we visited Fran was talking to the staff about their living conditions. She always wanted to know where and how people lived.

We had different interests but always ended the day to-gether. There is much that has happened in our lives, the deci-sions we made together, the support for what we wanted to do separately, the fun we had whenever we were together. Well that isn't totally true. I liked being with her but never enjoyed going shopping with her for "this season's wardrobe." I just think, "how strong we were as a twosome."

In this lifetime I have had jobs that were difficult and stress-ful while trying to satisfy customers and bosses and meeting schedules. They were jobs that I was paid to do. I now have an-other job that I am doing because I want to. It is also difficult and stressful at times, but I really can't fail for I am the expert here with years of experience and a dedication that can't be bought. And there is no one to fire me for not doing the work properly so I get a lot of practice. And every day I get better at it. I am taking care of the love of my life. I am doing the best I can at trying to make her life better and comfortable. I try and do the same for myself by adapting to Fran's needs with pa-tience. I think that is the major thing that I learned in dealing with this illness. Forget the clock and go with the flow. I figured out that Fran works best throughout the day on only two doses of her medicine. She seems more relaxed and is less anxious when this is what she takes. Her days seem easier for her and for anyone else who is with her.

So where are we now and what will we do? We will just keep on going on. I intend to take care of Fran as long as I can and sharing that responsibility with people I hire to be a care-giver for her. I intend to see that she is as comfortable as possi-ble and feels secure in her surroundings with the people who care for her as long as I can. And the reason for this is that I have a visceral love for this woman. She is my best friend. I look at her and long to be at her side. I always felt that way. If we were at some function where there was music being played I would only want to dance with her. When we were on hikes I only wanted to walk near her. When we were out eating I would love to sit next to her at the table and press my thigh against hers. I couldn't get enough of her. Even now, after I put Fran to bed at about seven in the evening, I complete the chores around the house. Washing up dishes, putting away laundry, doing some paper work or reading. I then go to bed and I usually wake Fran up and tell her "I'm here to bother you." And I do. I will kiss her cheek and scratch her head. She lies on her back and doesn't move much but she begins to smile. I know she is happy. It makes me happy. I will sometimes say something silly and she will laugh and so will I for a minute or so. And then in the morning when I wake up I take her hand in mine and we lay there holding hands. And I am happy that she is there. And I know that one day she will not be there and I will be heart broken, for a long time.